4,Bh

To Sue
with love from
Mom and Dad
Xmas '86

Photography by David Muench
Text by Michael Frome

The NATIONAL PARKS

RAND McNALLY & COMPANY
Chicago / New York / San Francisco

Contents

Photos on pages 8–9, 10 (top), 11
  by Bradford Washburn;
page 10 (bottom) by Niels-Henrick L. Andersen;
pages 147–49 by Fritz Henle;
pages 150–1 by R. Mason;
pages 152, 153 (bottom), 154–59
  from the National Park Service;
page 153 (top) by
  Stephen J. Krasemann / Alaska Photo

Library of Congress Cataloging in Publication Data

Muench, David
    THE NATIONAL PARKS

    1. National parks and reserves—United States.
I. Frome, Michael. II. Title.
E160.M93   917.3'04'92   77–4075

First printing, third edition, 1986

THE NATIONAL PARKS

The Search for Meaning

OR MORE THAN 30 YEARS I HAVE BEEN TRAVELING OUT AMONG THE NATIONAL PARKS, HIKING, camping, canoeing, kayaking, riding on horses and in automobiles; reporting on what the parks are like; and advising people how best to enjoy them. I have pursued the history and politics of national parks and the diverse arts and sciences they embody, and almost every day I learn something new about them.

All this time I have tried to determine in my own mind and heart the full meaning of these special places, not only to me as an individual and to my generation during our brief tenure of earth, but also to generations far beyond our own—for parks, after all, unlike generations, are forever.

I like to think that this book helps to place the parks in perspective. It has been extremely well received ever since the first edition appeared in 1977. I marveled then, and still do now, at the breathtaking photographs by David Muench; I could hardly have hoped for a better collaborator. His pictures capture the moods, the mystery, and the romance of America's treasures. They cannot fail to stimulate among readers a sense of pride and idealism, a desire and hope that these treasures endure as a continuing emblem of our civilization.

The book was praised by reviewers. It was given an award by the Geographic Society of Chicago. It was chosen as one of 100 books for display at the 1979 Moscow Book Fair to represent American life and landscape. More than one U.S. ambassador ordered copies to present as gifts to other nations.

I appreciate the Rand McNally commitment to excellence, manifest in the editing, production, and readiness to expand and update the book as needed. For parks, after all, are no more static than democracy. I've been to them many times over and am still learning what they mean and do for us.

By way of example, you might be interested in my travels during the summer of 1985. Starting in June from my home base at the University of Idaho, I went first to California. In Los Angeles, I visited Horace Marden Albright, aged 95, a venerable national parks pioneer and particular friend, in order to hear his recollections of early days. Then I toured Santa Monica Mountains National Recreation Area, a touch of nature in the Southern California megalopolis, and three national parks—Channel Islands, Sequoia and Kings Canyon, and Yosemite. At Sequoia and Kings Canyon I backpacked with a friend into the high reaches of the spectacular and isolated Mineral King Valley, added to the

park by Congress in 1978. Formerly national forestland, Mineral King had been considered for development as a huge mechanized ski resort. "Well, I don't know what God had in mind for this place," I said to my companion while overlooking the high peaks, lakes, and clear streams, "but it could hardly have been a Disney ski resort."

In July, I flew west across the Pacific to Hawaii Volcanoes National Park, where lava and cinder cones spewed from ancient and live volcanoes are reminders that the earth is still in charge of its own destiny. For the first time I climbed to the summit of Mauna Loa, elevation 13,677 feet, mostly over barren lava fields and along lava-splattered cracks made by the 1984 eruption. I was most impressed, however, by successful efforts of park personnel to eliminate feral goats and pigs that for years had overrun the park, devouring its vegetation and making life difficult if not impossible for native fauna, principally forest birds. This restoration of a natural scene proves that it can be done.

Then in August I went to Alaska, principally to Glacier Bay and Denali national parks. Twenty-five years ago, both were remote and only lightly visited, but now no longer. They are almost too easy to reach and need protection from becoming outdoor playgrounds.

Happily, in the national parks each person can still become aware of his small place in the universe and as part of the cosmic web of life. A national park offers a uniquely equipped setting where Americans can learn love and reverence for nature, and perhaps, through nature, for one another and for other living creatures as well. The human is the most highly evolved being, the only animal capable of bringing about massive environmental changes, but our species exists only by virtue of conditions created and maintained through the millennia by other forms of life.

President Theodore Roosevelt was among those who have touched the meaning of the national parks in the fullest, richest dimensions. In 1903, while traveling in California, he spent three days in Yosemite with John Muir. The first night they bedded down in fir boughs among giant trunks of ancient sequoias, listening to the hermit thrush and the waterfalls tumbling down the sheer cliffs. "It was like lying in a great solemn cathedral," wrote the president, "far vaster and more beautiful than any built by the hand of man."

Then, in a speech at Stanford University, Roosevelt demonstrated his deep interest in preserving, on lofty philosophical grounds, both the giant sequoias of the Sierra Nevada

and the coast redwoods:

"I feel most emphatically that we should not turn into shingles a tree which was old when the first Egyptian conqueror penetrated to the valley of the Euphrates, which it has taken so many thousands of years to build up, and which can be put to better use. That, you may say, is not looking at the matter from the practical standpoint. There is nothing more practical than the preservation of beauty, than the preservation of anything that appeals to the higher emotions of mankind."

National parks are predicated upon "the higher emotions of mankind." They represent not simply the marvels of the American continent—embodied in Yellowstone, Yosemite, Grand Canyon, Rocky Mountain, Glacier, Everglades, and other parks wrought by a hand older and stronger than man's—but the finest of the American spirit as well. Ours is a nation steeped in materialism, where earth usually is treated as a commodity to be bought and sold, explored and exploited, where personal wealth is measured by the accumulation of property and tangible possessions. Yet there is another side to our nation: the idealism abundantly manifest in the concept of the national parks.

"The national park idea represents a far-reaching cultural achievement, for here we raise our thoughts above the average, and enter a sphere in which the intangible values of the human heart and spirit take precedence."

Thus wrote Adolph Murie, who for years—until his death in 1975—conducted important wildlife ecological studies in the national parks. He and his brother Olaus were field naturalists who aimed at true research, conducting the kind of intimate, on-the-ground contact with animals that leads to a genuine understanding of nature. I encountered Adolph in Alaska and Wyoming and had close discussions with him. I felt he had a perception of park values far beyond that of almost everyone in or out of government.

In the national parks there is no harvesting of timber, no hunting of wild animals, no extraction of minerals (exept in a few unfortunate cases where mining rights predate the establishment of individual parks), and no grazing of domestic livestock. Trees are apt to be consumed by disease. Or by wildfire, left to run its course. Or blown down in a windstorm. By whatever cause, trees are left where they fall. This is nature's way. The dead or dying tree provides a home for insects, and these in turn draw birds to feed upon them. In time the tree will decompose to enrich the earth from whence it sprang. The burned-over area will become the source of a new forest destined to fulfill its cycle in time.

The national parks are life-museums, in which each wild species, whether plant or animal, large or small, possesses implicit scientific interest. Yellowstone is more than the photogenic spectaculars of Old Faithful and the paint pots; it's the grizzlies and other wild species and the whole life system and the unfenced danger of a pioneer earthscape.

Even without people the parks are valid. Whether he or she takes a pack or not, whether he or she ever sees or walks in the wilds, a man or woman can feel a little closer to eternity because somewhere a small part of earth's life has been granted its right to be. As long as beauty and grandeur of primitive scenery are preserved—just to *know* they are there—the primeval places will have an inspiring influence in shaping the character of people.

National parks are the landscape that poets and painters and all types of creative persons have drawn upon for generations. "Here are worlds of experience beyond the world of aggressive man, beyond history, beyond science," according to Ansel Adams, the modern laureate of Yosemite. And yet none of us can foresee the artistry still to be wrought in some future time.

Parks are not a new, nor even an American, creation. They were known in ancient civilizations and were recognized as a mark of advancement in the development of European countries. In the settlement of the New World, open squares, greens, and commons were set aside for community purposes. As cities grew, the city park system emerged with the establishment of Central Park in New York City in 1857. The landscape architect of the park, Frederick Law Olmsted, saw it as humanizing the city, softening its hard edges through nature.

The first action by the federal government came in 1832, when the U.S. Congress established a small reservation in Hot Springs, Arkansas. In 1864—even during the heat of the Civil War—Congress acted again; at the behest of prominent Americans, it set aside Yosemite Valley and the Mariposa Grove of Big Trees and gave them to California as a state park, a protection of priceless giant sequoias from the threat of commercial timber exploitation.

But it was six years later, in 1870, when the first basic step was taken for an entire nation to preserve its treasures unimpaired for future generations. Vast areas of the West

were being rapidly colonized while still unknown country was being explored. Yet on this raw, fast-developing land the expression "national park" appears to have been used for the first time in the sense we know it today.

It happened that the Washburn-Langford-Doane expedition had set out from Fort Ellis, Montana, on August 21, 1870, to explore and document the wonders of the fabulous Yellowstone country. By September 19 the party had covered an amazing amount of ground, discovering, naming, and mapping features, including Old Faithful. Around a campfire the men discussed what to do with their find. According to law, they could have laid claim for personal gain. Instead they decided that such treasures belong by higher right to all people. They envisioned a permanent preserve and then campaigned for it. Two years later Yellowstone was established by Congress as the first national park—the first anywhere.

Establishing the park by law did not guarantee its lasting integrity; somehow it never does, except with constant public vigilance. At Yellowstone, because of scant appropriations there were not enough rangers to patrol an area almost as large as Connecticut. Only 14 years after the park had been designated it became necessary to summon the U.S. Cavalry to protect its resources from game poachers, loggers, trappers, and miners. And the Army stayed for 30 years.

In the years following, other parks were established, and by 1907 there were eight. New laws were passed, such as the Antiquities Act of 1906, protecting ancient cliff dwellings and pueblos of the Southwest and "other objects of scientific interest," which included fossil remains as well. Then in 1916, the Organic Act created a new federal agency, the National Park Service. It declared that the purpose of national parks, monuments, and reservations would be "to conserve the scenery and the natural and historic objects and the wild life therein and to provide for the enjoyment of the same in such manner and by such means as will leave them unimpaired for the enjoyment of future generations."

Since then the National Park Service and the system it administers have grown into a vital force in American life, developed still further in 1980 to embrace seven new parks in Alaska. The wonders of the 48 national parks covered in this book range from the underground worlds of Carlsbad Caverns, Wind Cave, and Mammoth Cave to the hardwood Appalachian forests of Shenandoah and Great Smoky Mountains and the western evergreen forests of Olympic, Redwood, and Sequoia and Kings Canyon; from the subtropical wonder-

land of Everglades, the cliff dwellings of Mesa Verde, and the living desert of Big Bend to the glaciers of North Cascades, Glacier, and Mount Rainier; from the geological spectacles of Zion, Bryce, Capitol Reef, Canyonlands, and the Grand Canyon to the wildlife of Yellowstone, Rocky Mountain, Denali, and Gates of the Arctic.

The national parks are now only part of the total National Park System, embracing more than 330 separate units and almost 80 million acres. These include archaeological areas of the early Americans; historical areas like Jamestown, Independence Hall, and Gettysburg Battlefield; national monuments, national seashores, national parkways, national preserves, national rivers, and national recreation areas like mammoth Lake Mead, nearly 2 million rugged acres of tawny deserts, deep canyons, and lofty plateaus.

These protected areas constitute a gallery of American treasures—treasures that inspire, instruct, and stimulate spiritual well-being. They are an endowment of riches that makes the United States the envy of the world. In fact, more than 90 nations around the world now have their own systems of national parks. Large portions of the most famous islands in the world, the Galápagos, are protected in a national park. So are the great game ranges in Africa. And so too is one-fifth of the obscure little island of Bonaire in the Netherlands Antilles, named Washington National Park. All these parks the world over stem from the idea conceived at the Yellowstone campfire of 1870. Such is America's export of idealism.

Nature is the oldest thing on earth, but nature reserves are among the youngest. Nations still don't understand all the things such reserves can do, or how to use them properly and fully. Certainly these places must figure in the search for an environmental ethic. Considering that we must come to terms with nature to survive, national parks can be expected to serve as models of respect for the land around us.

My fervent hope is that this new edition of *The National Parks* will provide many Americans with visual enjoyment, reading pleasure, and guidance, or, perhaps, inspiration in the search for meaning. In our age of supertechnology and overpopulation—of supercivilization—the preservation of nature provides spiritual sustenance, an ethic of self-worth and self-renewal.

THE NORTHWEST & ALASKA

Denali National Park

THE IMMENSE SANCTUARY OF SPECTACULARS CALLED DENALI NATIONAL PARK, 250 MILES SOUTH of the Arctic Circle, is a marvel of the planet and a national park if ever one was meant to be.

Mount McKinley—or Denali, "the high one," as early Indians called it—dominates the stark landscape. Often it is shrouded in clouds, but when the skies open I can see the towering mass of snow and ice from any part of the park. It rises 20,320 feet, to the highest point on this continent. There are other major peaks, like Mount Foraker, 17,400 feet, also taller than anything in the "lower 48," and many glaciers 30 and 40 miles long.

The wildlife compares with that in the famous game parks of East Africa in variety of species and abundance of numbers. Here in Denali I can observe America's native reindeer, the barren-ground caribou. The concentration of huge herds of hundreds, sometimes of thousands, advancing in migration across the tundra spurs me to dream of what the rest of the land was like before man claimed it. Denali is one of the last strongholds of wolves and grizzly bears, species that symbolize untamed nature. On rugged high slopes I spot a band of Dall sheep, the northern white sheep, sure-footed climbers distinguished by massive horns that curl a full circle or more.

Reflecting on Denali, I find my thoughts turning to people of a special breed, north country people who love the park and give themselves to it.

My friend Charles J. Ott is one of this breed. He might have become known as one of the world's foremost wildlife photographers, but was content to work as a maintenance man on the national park staff for many years until retiring in 1974 (when he moved into a cabin near the park). Even though he was on the government payroll, he would never fail to speak out on behalf of the wild environment and against projects that would disrupt it. His photographs of wild animals have been widely published, and I have never seen any better. Charlie's pictures come from his love for the animals and from his effort to do them justice. He would follow a lynx for hours to get the right picture without disturbing the big bobtailed cat of the north.

Once Charlie and a friend spent a whole day on snowshoes looking for lynx, without seeing a fresh track. It was about 20 below zero and their cameras weren't working right. They went back to Charlie's place, where park personnel live, to get some coffee to warm their innards. Charlie looked out the window and suddenly saw three lynx. Both men grabbed

AERIAL VIEW OF MOUNT McKINLEY

their cameras, ran outside, and followed the lynx up the hill and into the willows—without jackets, gloves, or caps. "We never got a chance for even a long shot," he would lament later. "And we were icicles when we got back!"

Then there was Adolph Murie, the federal field biologist, who wrote books on the birds and mammals of Alaska unlike any others the government ever published, books filled with rich prose and perceptions, illustrated with wildlife sketches by his brother Olaus and with photographs by Charlie Ott. Above all, these classic books are based on his own long years of intimate research.

Adolph studied grizzlies closely. Wherever he would camp there were grizzlies, wandering freely over their ranges, feeding on green vegetation and digging for roots. He learned to burn his garbage and food containers to destroy odors and consequently never had bear trouble. Adolph's lesson was: If you keep your faith—and a respectable distance—wilderness recreation and grizzlies are compatible.

He was virtually on speaking terms with wolves, listening to their howls floating softly across the tundra, watching them hunting singly and in packs, edging to their dens so closely that he once withdrew two pups without stirring protest. Once, while traveling on skis, he watched foxes, wolves, and wolverines feeding on the hind leg of a moose. Last to eat? It was the foxes, who curled up and waited until the others finished.

When Mount McKinley National Park was established in 1917, more than half the mountain was left outside the park's boundaries. Also unprotected were critical wildlife habitats on the tundra plains and in the boreal forest. For years Adolph Murie urged enlarging the park to insure animals "ample room for carrying on their living in a natural, free manner." This plea has been realized at last: Denali National Park and bordering Denali National Preserve now cover 5,696,000 acres (more than twice the size of the former park alone), correcting long-standing deficiencies and embracing the spectacular Cathedral Spires. It is truly one of the finest wildlife preserves on earth.

North Cascades National Park

GOING INTO THE SOUTH UNIT OF NORTH CASCADES NATIONAL PARK REMINDS ME OF GOING to Isle Royale, the island national park in Michigan. An automobile is neither required nor useful. The best way to get to both is by boat. There the similarity ends, for the trip into the Cascades aboard the *Lady of the Lake* is an adventure in itself, and I know of nothing else like it in America.

It is more like a voyage on a Swiss lake. In fact, the passenger ferry starts from the town of Chelan and stops at Lucerne on its 50-mile course to the head of Lake Chelan. The trip also calls to mind similar ones in the heart of the Bavarian Alps, especially on the Königsee at Berchtesgaden.

The North Cascades have been called "the American Alps," and even while approaching the range by boat I understand why. The breathtaking alpine scenery encompasses what the Swiss would describe as spectacular pinnacles, massifs, ridges, and cols, flanked by glaciers and snowfields feeding cirque lakes and streams in high meadows. This national park in northern Washington preserves almost a thousand square miles of virtually untouched landscape, the most dramatic section of the entire Cascade Range. The park consists of two separate units, the North Unit bordering on Canada.

I land at Stehekin, the little settlement at the head of the lake and at the outlet of the Stehekin River. It would not be too painful to live here forever. For the moment, however, Stehekin serves as the point to hire a ride over the narrow road along the river, passing the trails that lead up Agnes Creek, Bridge Creek, and Park Creek to the road's end at Cottonwood Camp.

Cottonwood is the beginning of the steep trail to 5,392-foot-high Cascade Pass. On top I find a fantastic outlook ringed by glaciers and snowfields, by Boston Peak, Sahale Mountain, and 8,966-foot-high Mount Logan and 8,868-foot-high Mount Eldorado beyond them. The Hudsonian meadows at hand are colored by the flowers of lovely and rare plants, such as the lamb's-tongue fawn lily, and the glacier lily, with its golden-yellow blossom. The glacier lily is not as well known as the avalanche fawn lily, its larger and more abundant cousin—mainly because it blooms early, when the snow melts—but it's a jewel of the high places nonetheless.

It seems strange that such marvels of the landscape as the American Alps should be so little known outside their immediate region. The North Cascades are a range of giant faults and massive overthrusts, mostly between

SAHALE MOUNTAIN, MAGIC MOUNTAIN, AND BONANZA PEAK

LIBERTY BELL MOUNTAIN AND WASHINGTON PASS

GLACIER LILIES

8,000 and 9,000 feet in elevation. Formed of durable granites and related rocks, the northern mountains have held out longer against weathering than the Southern Cascades, which are formed of the softer lavas, accounting for the sharp peaks and knife-edge passes. But with the immense amount of precipitation from some of the continent's wettest prevailing winds, relentlessly grinding ice has taken its toll of the North Cascades, shearing off ridges and carving cirques, canyons, and valleys.

For many years the North Cascades were administered as part of the national forests. Proposals were made from time to time to recognize the superlative quality of the region through establishment of a national park, centered on Mount Baker, 10,778 feet high, northernmost of the chain of the great volcanic cones of the Cascades, and its dramatic neighbor, Mount Shuksan, 9,127 feet high. But there seemed to be little imperative to preserve this harsh, almost impenetrable land—at least not until the 1950s with the advent of chain saws, bulldozers, and logging trucks.

Outdoors enthusiasts were concerned with saving the low-country virgin forests as respectful entryways to high-country meadows, glaciers, and peaks. Instead, logging equipment overrode watershed soils, scraping stream bottoms and silting fisheries. Tons of debris called "slash" were burned, covering the woods with a pall of smoke; sometimes the fires got out of hand and spread.

Finally a nationwide campaign was launched, and this led to action by Congress, which in 1968 established this new national park "in order to preserve for the benefit, use, and inspiration of present and future generations certain majestic mountain scenery, snow fields, glaciers, alpine meadows and other unique natural features in the North Cascade Mountains."

Ross Lake National Recreation Area separates the national park into two units, and Lake Chelan National Recreation Area adjoins the South Unit of the park. The two recreation areas, centered around the deep, fjord-like lakes, focus on such activities as camping, boating, fishing, and hunting; the national park units, on the other hand, are dedicated to preservation, including preservation of mountain goats, deer, bears, moose, wolverines, and all other forms of wildlife. Both the recreation areas and the park are endowed with beauty and solitude. Between the moisture-laden forests of the west side and the open sunny woods of the east, plant communities range from subalpine conifers through green meadows to alpine tundra, then back down to pine forests and dry shrub lands.

The North Unit embraces some of the Cascades' finest glaciers, granite peaks, high lakes, and remote valleys on the slopes of Mount Challenger and the other peaks of the rugged Picket Range and of Mount Shuksan. Mount Baker still lies outside the boundaries of the park. In the almost 700 miles of the Cascade chain, only Lassen Peak in California and Mount Rainier in Washington are protected within national parks. Unfinished business, I would call it.

MOUNT SHUKSAN

Olympic National Park

MOISTURE IS EVERYWHERE IN THE HOH VALLEY. WHEN WATER ISN'T FALLING AS rain, it drips from tree limbs and leaves or from mist in the air. Consequently the vegetation is well watered and luxuriant. The Hoh is one of those rare, enchanting botanical wonderlands that demonstrate the genius of nature preserved.

I walk through the Valley wearing raincoat and waterproof boots. The Hoh is one of the gardens called "rain forests" along the west slope of the Olympic Peninsula of Washington State, once the "upper left-hand corner" of the United States. The year-round climate is mild but humid, and winter is wetter here than in any other part of the nation outside Alaska. The Hoh and the other rain-forest valleys, Bogachiel, Queets, and Quinault, are so lush that they comprise the entire sweep of plant progression from humble fungi, mosses, and lichens to immense evergreen trees 300 feet high and a thousand years old.

Many notable forests grow along the Pacific Ocean from Alaska to California, including stands of redwoods, the world's tallest trees. I daresay, however, that none is more productive than the Olympic rain forests with their thousand species of plants. Olympic National Park is plainly a sanctuary for plants, many of them threatened elsewhere.

The west side of the Peninsula is fertile because it stands first in line to meet the Pacific. The open peaks of the Olympic Mountains wring rain, snow, and mist from the west winds. Then waters rush down from glaciers and snowfields toward their outlet to the sea. The east side, in contrast, is quite dry.

In the Hoh Valley, soft green light filters through translucent leaves and bounces from one surface to another. Mosses cover rocks; some mosses grow like air plants, draped in fragile beauty from the limbs and tops of trees, cushioned with arched trunks of vine maple. Still other mosses grow with sword fern, Oregon oxalis, and bead-ruby across the forest floor, a thick carpet formed of decaying organic matter with a thriving population of mice, shrews, salamanders, and insects. Mosses and lichens cover fallen old trees that serve as nurseries, or "nurse logs," for spruce and hemlock seedlings, which prefer rotting wood.

With conditions favorable since the last Ice Age, Olympic valleys have bloomed with evergreen giants. In the Hoh I can identify the "big four" of the Olympic Peninsula—the western red cedar, reaching heights of 175 feet, with cinnamon-red fibrous bark and flat, lacy sprays of almost fernlike leaves; the western hemlock, a little smaller, with russet-brown bark and abundant, very short cones at the ends of its branches, a tree that imparts a sense of dignity; the Sitka spruce, lordly and energetic, towering over most other trees, easily recognized by its sharp, silvery-green needles. And then there is the Douglas fir, mightiest of all, exceeded in size only by the redwood and *Sequoia gigantea* among all the trees on the continent. The strength and quality of its wood has made it a choice source of sawtimber, so that little remains in virgin condition outside the national parks. In Olympic National Park I can still see stately and wonderfully proportioned Douglas fir trees that have already lived 400 to 1,000 years, looking down at the world from heights of 250 to 300 feet.

Olympic National Park was established in 1938. The narrow strip along the ocean, away from the much larger section to the east, was added in 1953, and extended in 1976.

There is far more to the grand 908,000-acre park than rain forests, of course. Here one finds the classic high-mountain Western wilderness, alpine lakes, rushing rivers and streams, abundant wildlife, remoteness and solitude. The 50-mile-long coastal strip embraces the most primitive coast south of Canada.

At Hurricane Ridge, on the north side of the park, I look up at a mighty glacial world surrounding the Bailey Range and 7,965-foot Mount Olympus, half hidden in clouds, where the ice is as much as 900 feet thick. Hiking out to Mount Angeles through the wildflower-carpeted meadows of Heather Park, then climbing among the rocky crags, I catch sight of mountain goats, black-tailed deer, and the Olympic marmot, or "whistler," a distinct species that lives only here. From a mile above the sea, I look across the Strait of Juan de Fuca to Vancouver Island and inland to Mount Baker and to the Skagit Range across the Canadian border.

Another day, hiking the High Divide Trail from Sol Duc Hot Springs, I climb past the splashing waters of Soleduck Falls and cross the Seven Lakes Basin, a lovely high cirque above the Bogachiel River. To the north lies Lake Crescent, the largest lake in the park, a place of beauty from any angle. I am conscious of signs of elk. In the rain forest I have seen their footprints in hardened mud, their teeth marks on browsed trees and shrubs, and telltale pellets in clusters on the ground to show where they have been. Along the trail I catch sight of a band of about 30 elk obviously summering in the high country, moving across a meadow perhaps to drink at one of the lakes; they are large animals of their kind, mostly brownish in color. I am reminded that this area was first set aside as a national monument to protect wildlife, particularly the Roosevelt, or Olympic, elk, and that here the largest remaining herd roams free.

Finally I walk along the sandy beaches and steep headlands of the coastal strip, where waters complete their cycle to the sea. I walk with the spirit of Fred Overly, a friend who is gone; as park superintendent he was instrumental years ago in acquiring this tract, without which the park would be incomplete. Persistent waves and the encroaching sea sculpture tree-studded islands, rocky arches, and crescent beaches. Sea lions and other seals find their sanctuary on the rocks and frolic in the water. Gulls, crows, oyster catchers, and cormorants enliven sky and water; colorful hydroids, sea urchins, and anemones bedeck the tidal pools. The land-and-sea cosmos is vibrant with life and learning.

HEMLOCK

HOH VALLEY RAIN FOREST

WHENEVER I FLY TO SEATTLE FROM THE EAST, OR FROM SOMEWHERE SOUTH ON THE Pacific coast, I watch for Mount Rainier on the descent. At this distance, some 60 miles southeast of the city, its summit resembles a massive vanilla ice cream cone—the ice cream part without the cone. Actually, about 40 square miles of icy glacial rivers cap Rainier, the loftiest volcanic peak of the Cascade Range, a gleaming 14,410-foot landmark visible for hundreds of miles when the weather is clear.

From the air the Cascades don't look quite the same as when I first saw them, or as I dreamed they would. To me the Cascades have always been a high wave of Western green glory, unbroken except for the distinctive volcanic summits that whiten the horizon with a perpetual cover of snow. Now, as I look down from the airplane window, I see the telltale signs of modern logging in the huge brown open blocks checkerboarding the green. Each time I visit the Northwest there are more blocks, or "clear-cuts," and less visual beauty. Then I look at the forests around the base of Mount Rainier and am glad for what has been saved.

So many areas these days are accessible and conquerable, whether forests to loggers or mountains to climbers. It is difficult to sustain the respect, love, and reverence that nature deserves. Imagine, in contrast, the emotions swelling within Philomen Beecher Van Trump on his first view of Mount Rainier in August, 1867, from a prairie southeast of Olympia. Fortunately he recorded his feelings, as follows:

"The first true vision of the mountain, revealing so much of its glorious beauty and grandeur, its mighty and sublime form filling up nearly all the field of direct vision, swelling up from the plain and out of the green forest till its lofty triple summit towered immeasurably above the picturesque foothills, the westering sun flooding with golden light and softening tints its lofty summit, rugged sides and far-sweeping flanks—all this impressed me so indescribably, enthused me so thoroughly, that I then and there vowed almost with fervency that I would someday stand upon its glorious summit, if that feat were possible to human effort and endurance."

Three years later he proved that the feat was possible. Van Trump and General Hazard Stevens were guided by Sluiskin, a Yakima Indian, to a point near the top of the peak. The Indian warned against going any higher, but they persisted and went on alone, making the first recorded ascent of the summit. Presently their lives were endangered by the cold

INDIAN PAINTBRUSH AND BLEACHED ROOTS

and windy weather of late afternoon, but they found sanctuary for the night in an area warmed by jets of steam blowing through cracks in the rocks. "Strong men, stout hearts," Sluiskin greeted them in the Indian tongue on their return.

In 1888 Van Trump guided John Muir to the top of Mount Rainier. Muir was enthusiastic about the superlative quality of this kingdom of glaciers. Following strong public campaigning, the national park was established in 1899 from lands formerly part of the large Mount Rainier Forest Reserve. Curiously, forest reserves had been set aside in the 1890s from the public domain so they could no longer

be claimed and patented for private ownership. The objective was to protect the high watersheds and forests for the long-range public good, and this principle prevailed long after the reserves were redesignated as national forests. In the national parks the early concept was to preserve spectacular features, yet make them accessible. But in the national forests, with little road building and conservative logging, the wilderness remained extensive and challenging—that is, until the 1960s, when the emphasis shifted to large-scale tree-cutting.

At Mount Rainier, the dynamic forces that create and shape the land are starkly evident, for the broad dome embraces the most extensive "single-peak" glacial system in the United States outside of Alaska. The Emmons is the largest of Rainier's many glaciers, and the Carbon is the longest. Its 40-square-mile expanse of glaciers makes Rainier something more than a national park; it is also a classroom in volcanism, soil formation, erosion, glaciation, flooding, and the effects of climate and of climate changes.

Rainier's summit is often obscured by clouds and fog resulting from a natural cycle of westerly Pacific winds rising to pass over the mountains and then cooling, with the condensing moisture falling as rain or snow. Snows are very heavy; during the 1971–72 winter a world's record of 1,122 inches was recorded at Paradise, 5,500 feet high, and

doubtless much more fell at higher elevations, where measurements cannot be made.

A glacier forms where snowfalls exceed melting; once formed, it moves downhill by virtue of its own weight, like a river of ice. On the flanks of Mount Rainier I study the fascinating blue-green crevasses and seracs of Nisqually Glacier. Advancing about 50 to 400 feet per year—the rate varies at different levels—Nisqually churns and moves the earth's mantle, rasping the firm rock in its path and leaving it smooth. It carries away the plowed-off and filed-off debris. I hear the rumble of ice crashing into a stream milky with glacial snow. And at the barren terminus of the glacier the humblest plants move in to start building new soil.

MOUNT RAINIER AND LAKE GEORGE

Everywhere I look there are blossoms, right up to the edge of the snowbank, and sometimes even in the snow. At lower elevations, in the valleys around the base of the mountain, the heavy moisture produces a luxuriant growth of dense forests dominated by the great trees of the Northwest, including Douglas fir, western hemlock, western red cedar, and Sitka spruce, with ferns, brackens, and flowers carpeting the floor beneath them. Between 4,000 and 6,500 feet I hike the Wonderland Trail at the foot of glaciers through meadows carpeted with paintbrush, lupine, mountain buttercup, and avalanche lily and through open stands of hemlock, Alaska cedar, and subalpine fir.

Above 6,500 feet rock, snow, and ice prevail. Most of the year Rainier lies under snow. In the brief summer the high country belongs to the mountain goats, moving in bands along the rocky crags between ice and snow, and to the mountain climbers challenging unstable rock, heavily crevassed glaciers, sudden storms, and freezing high winds. One difference between goat and man is that the former has adapted naturally to this harsh environment, whereas man has conditioned and trained himself and introduced sophisticated equipment and clothing. Within the past ten years the number of climbers has increased 300 percent.

Nature is not flawless, as evidenced on Rainier by fallen timber streaking the slopes where avalanches thundered down, but it's always natural, and that makes it right. At Reflection Lake and Louise Lake, along the Stevens Canyon Road, I can see Mount Rainier mirrored like a landscape painting and to the south the peaks of the rugged Tatoosh Range, with glacier-clad 12,326-foot Mount Adams towering behind them. I am within the "glorious beauty and grandeur" that inspired Van Trump. If I should be here on a day when everything is obscured by clouds and fog, I know they may quickly dissipate, leaving the peak bathed in sunlight. And if not, there will always be another day.

MOUNT RAINIER

OVERLEAF: REFLECTION LAKE >

Crater Lake National Park

ELIBERATELY RISING EARLY, I HIKE TO THE RIM OF CRATER LAKE AND ARRIVE IN A DEAD heat with daybreak. At this hour the water is calm and mirrorlike, affording a superlative reflection of the peaks rising above it. There is not another soul in sight. I luxuriate in having this serene landscape all to myself, at least for this magic moment.

Crater Lake, cradled within the basin of Mount Mazama, embodies beauty and wonder, exercising a wholly beneficial influence on all who see it. I can understand why it was once called "Lake Majesty," a name that would still be fitting today. For a brief instant I think of other American lakes that fall in the class of paradise lost. Here the entire park—protected since 1902, when it was established—has retained much of the original wilderness charter, not solely in its deep blue lake but also in its entire cosmos of green meadows, forests, canyons, streams, and pumice desert flats.

The national park lies in the Cascades, a province abounding in mountain lakes, alpine meadows, and snowcapped volcanic peaks such as Mount Hood, Three Sisters, and Mount Jefferson. Mount Hood, in northern Oregon, is a marvelous area, thronged with winter skiers. The scene at Crater Lake, in the southern portions of the Cascades in Oregon, is different. Crater Lake is the treasure preserved, free of logging scars, road networks, and ski lifts. Heavy snowfalls cloak the evergreens, creating a glistening landscape of solitude and beauty.

While standing at the edge of the lake I try to visualize the forces that created this scene, to comprehend the full geological drama of this extinct volcano amidst the lava cliffs. I try to conceive it more firmly from different points along the 25-mile rim and looking down from some of the peaks.

Apparently Mount Mazama once towered above glacier-filled valleys and forested foothills. Then, about 7,000 years ago, Mazama erupted. Instead of the mountain just blowing its top, the shell remaining collapsed and fell inward, forming an immense basin 20 square miles in area surrounded by towering walls rising 500 to 2,000 feet above the water, a formation called a "caldera." An avalanche of fiery rock and lava spread destruction well beyond it, much like the violent eruption of Mount St. Helens in 1980.

The lake is the deepest in the United States (almost 2,000 feet). In the Western Hemisphere only Great Slave Lake in Canada is deeper. There are other calderas, other lakes in volcanic cones, but none of this magnitude or with these dimensions. Oddly, the lake

has neither inlet nor outlet, but the water accumulated from rain and snow remains relatively constant by seepage.

At Cleetwood Cove I walk down the mile-long trail to the water's edge, where I join the boat tour that circles the lake close to the caldera walls. A park naturalist aboard interprets the geology of the multicolored igneous rock. Phantom Ship, rising dramatically above the surface, is clearly a formation of volcanic rock. Wizard Island suggests that the volcanic action leading to Mazama's collapse did not die at once; there must have been sufficient activity left to produce this volcano within a volcano that rises about 760 feet above the surface, and there may be other cones beneath it.

I learn that there may actually have been human witnesses to the fireworks long ago. Legends of the Klamath Indians refer to this area as "battleground of the gods" and tell of earth-shattering explosions and mountains that spewed fire, caused by the "Chief of the Below World." And Indian artifacts have been unearthed in parts of central Oregon beneath pumice ejected from Mount Mazama. Imagine the terrifying thoughts racing through the minds of early people as clouds of smoke and volcanic ash blotted the sun from the sky. But are we much better prepared to confront natural catastrophe, even with scientific warning systems? Or do we rely too strongly on science, inviting catastrophe by building on known earthquake fault lines and on the floodplains of rivers that must ultimately overflow their banks?

Crater Lake is a special place to learn nature's mechanisms. Because of its purity, the lake has been designated a "national hydrologic benchmark" for scientific study. Its purity influences the incredibly brilliant azure blue color, long a subject of speculation. Some thought it a reflection of the sky, yet the color remains the same whether the sky is clear or clouded. Mineral content perhaps? The naturalist dips a small amount of water out of the lake, showing it to be as clear as any other water. He then adds that chemical analysis reveals no special content. Now it's believed that the clarity of the water allows light to penetrate the depths, where rays of other colors are absorbed; only the blue rays are reflected to the surface.

Above the rim I hike among the Cascadian pines, firs, and hemlocks to obtain lofty views above the lake. The Watchman, on the west rim, opens vistas in all directions, even to Mount Shasta, 100 miles south in California. Across the lake, I climb past Cloudcap between snowbanks and thick stands of whitebark pine to Mount Scott, the highest point

in the park, almost 2,800 feet above the lake. Along the way I encounter ground squirrels, which seem to be everywhere (at least everywhere that humans walk), chipmunks, and yellow-bellied marmots among the rockslides. Jays and nutcrackers are prevalent too, particularly along the rim, though many other species of birds frequent the lake as well as other parts of the park.

The sections away from the lake are a revelation in themselves. In the southeast

WIZARD ISLAND IN CRATER LAKE

stand the Pinnacles, spired and fluted columns formed when loose volcanic fragments solidified around gas and steam vents. Within the canyons of Annie Creek and its tributaries I find additional pinnacles and unusual columnar-jointed scoria. One afternoon on the plateau dominated by Matterhorn-shaped Union Peak, in the southwest part, I catch sight of small herds of elk and dark black-tailed deer. Though not especially known for its wildlife, this national park provides sanc-

tuary for eagles and falcons and the beautiful Cascade red fox, coyotes, cougar, and other species.

In the northwestern section of the park, Sphagnum Bog is a rare phenomenon of the entire region. Its flora consists of mosses and herbs and several species of insect-eating plants, a community of frail natural balance, fed by Crater Springs. Boundary Springs, at the park's northern border, also supports a delicate moss and herb flora.

The water springs unexpectedly from an otherwise arid area, splashing downhill to join streams that form the Rogue River. From here in the high Cascades the wild Rogue—"the most beautiful stream of Oregon, the coldest, deepest, swiftest stream I ever fished," Zane Grey called it—flows more than 200 miles to meet the Pacific at Gold Beach. Having once boated the primitive portion between Grants Pass and Agness, I hope one day to trace the river the entire length of its course.

WHITEBARK PINE OVERLOOKING CRATER LAKE

CALIFORNIA & HAWAII

Lassen Volcanic National Park

A TRIP TO LASSEN VOLCANIC NATIONAL PARK IN HEAVILY WOODED NORTHEASTERN California, where the Sierra Nevada meets the Cascades, reminds me anew that geology is a living, active force. Hiking among the steaming fumaroles, hissing hot springs, and boiling mud pots and among the cones, craters, and vents that dot the park, I can hardly help but wonder: Where and when will the next violent outburst take place? Somehow, I'm sure, it will come.

My favorite section of Lassen Volcanic is the Cinder Cone, at an elevation of almost 7,000 feet, near the northeast corner of the park. Black in color and bare of vegetation, the steep-sided, cylindrical cone rises 700 feet above its base. It is surrounded by the Painted Dunes—red, gray, orange, and yellow-brown heaps of volcanic cinder and ash. Directly below lie the Fantastic Lava Beds, a mass of rough blocky black lava that originated when the cone erupted in 1850–51. That was its last hurrah (at least so far), when it was believed to be the source of "fires" and "flaring lights" seen as far off as 160 miles.

Near the southwest corner of the park, and just east of Little Hot Springs Valley, lies another favorite spot: sulfur-stained, crater-shaped Bumpass Hell, named for a pioneer who plunged a leg into the steaming mud and lived to regret it. Bumpass Hell is a wild arena of bubbling mud pots, rising steam, and hissing vents bearing such names as Big Boiler and the Steam Engine, all testifying to underground turbulence, part of the earth's endless activity. On the west side of Little Hot Springs Valley is the Sulphur Works, a seething array of gases and heat emitted from the caldera of ancient Mount Tehama.

Tehama was once a mighty mountain, 12 miles in diameter at its base. At the Sulphur Works I try to visualize the massive peak that would have towered 4,000 feet above me, the volcanic action, and the collapse of the top, which created a great bowl, or caldera. Looking west, I see the largest remnant of this old crater rim: the precipitous sheared side of Broke Off Mountain. Three miles to the north, I see Lassen Peak. Now *it* is the towering mass, though about a thousand feet lower than old Tehama. Lassen began as lava squeezed upward on the slope of Tehama. Too thick to flow like liquid, the lava plugged the vent from which it came and formed a rough, rounded mass called a "plug dome."

Lassen bears the name of a Danish immigrant, Peter Lassen, who came to the United States in 1830 looking for roving room. He found it in the high country east of Redding,

California, where even in summer the snow is apt to fall lightly on blue lakes and evergreen forests. Lassen Peak rises 10,457 feet, part of the fraternity of volcanic giants of the Pacific Northwest that includes Mount Baker, Mount Rainier, and Mount St. Helens in Washington, Mount Hood and Mount Mazama (of Crater Lake) in Oregon, and Mount Shasta in California. Ever since the white man moved west there has been volcanic activity somewhere in this chain of peaks, but until recent times the mountain named for Peter Lassen slumbered peacefully.

Nevertheless, the geology of the area was studied closely. In 1907, President Theodore Roosevelt signed a proclamation setting aside Cinder Cone and Lassen Peak as national monuments. Could anyone then have foreseen what was soon to come?

In the spring of 1914, after at least 400 years of quiet slumber, Lassen Peak started a series of eruptions that would continue for seven years. On May 30 a great column of steam and gases spouted from the top of the peak. The fireworks were on. Lassen erupted

more than 150 times during the first year alone, spouting dust and steam, flinging cinders and boulders. These were only the opening acts. In May, 1915, the big show began. Tongues of red lava spilled through a notch in the crater rim, flowed down the western slope 1,000 feet, and hardened in place. On the northeast flank, hot lava melting the deep snowpack caused a mammoth river of mud to rush downhill, carrying 30-ton boulders in its path. Three days later a column of vapor and dust rose more than five miles in the sky. Visible for at least 50 miles, it showered volcanic ash that ultimately came to rest in areas as distant as Nevada. A low-angle blast struck the northeast flank again. Five-ton rock bombs were catapulted into the air. The unleashed masses of gas-charged volcanic ash raced down the mountain, widening the path of destruction to more than a mile and mowing down trees and all other life in its path for a length of about five miles.

At the Devastated Area I observe the consequence of the "Great Hot Blast" and the mudflows. Trees were uprooted and broken

SIERRA SNOW PLANT

off like matchsticks; the area was completely denuded of growing forests. Now, however, blown-down trees have decayed to support new vegetation, including the beginning of a young pine forest. "Devastated Area" is a vivid descriptive place-name, but is it really a valid one for a phenomenon in the grand cycle of nature?

The eruptions of 1915 drew nationwide attention and led to the establishment of the national park a year later. The upheavals gradually declined, though small explosions continued until 1921. The crucible has long since cooled, and Lassen Peak, only recently upstaged by another newly active volcano in the continental United States, again wears its cap of long-lasting snow.

Yet just north of Lassen Peak at Chaos Crags I can see the future, or what appears to be the future, taking shape. The Crags appear as four domes occupying an area of about two square miles at altitudes up to 8,500 feet, maintaining a lonely vigil high above Manzanita Lake. Like Lassen Peak, the Crags are towering pluglike masses pushed up through vents a few thousand years ago. The second dome, on the northwest side, bears a large scar thought to be the source of the hummocky and furrowed Chaos Jumbles below it.

A first impression might be that the strewn rocky debris of the Jumbles was deposited through volcanic explosions. Close inspection, however, has shown that the Jumbles were created by great rockslides about three centuries ago. And now the Crags may be ready to give way again. In 1974 a geologist discovered instability of the rocks and cliffs, the threat of a potential avalanche that could bury everything in its path. As a result, the National Park Service closed the public facilities at Manzanita Lake. The campground was closed too, though a section was later reopened.

What next? The eruption of Mount St. Helens is a reminder that the Northwest has been the scene of earthly cataclysms over millions of years. St. Helens has seldom gone longer than 100 to 150 years between eruptions. With volcanic activity at Lassen as recent as 1921, possibly there will be new eruptions, the intrusion of another dome, or perhaps another mudflow like the one that occurred during the 1915 upheavals. One thing is certain: the earth won't remain the same.

Manzanita Lake is one of the park's treasure spots. Willow and alder dip their roots into the clear waters, and behind them lofty firs and pines ring the lake. I enjoy going to the high mountain meadows in early summer, when the paintbrush, lupine, penstemon, showy red Sierra snow plant, and other wild flowers are in bloom, and to the timberline, where weatherworn whitebark pine struggles to survive. I would also love to arrive in the still of winter to ski on the high, timber-free slopes and to listen to the fumaroles and boiling mud and watch the roaring steam.

TIMBERLINE ON LASSEN PEAK >

Redwood National Park

THE REDWOODS GROW IN DENSE GROVES IN THE MOISTURE-RICH FOG BELT ALONG THE PACIFIC coast, from the Santa Lucia Mountains below Carmel, California, to the Chetco River in southwestern Oregon. They grow nowhere else on earth. I have followed them north, starting from Santa Cruz on Monterey Bay, near their southern limit.

First, on the San Lorenzo River, there is Henry Cowell Redwoods State Park with a rather formidable grove. The Giant Tree in this park has been measured at 285 feet in height and 51 feet in circumference. Then there is Big Basin Redwoods State Park, the first preserve of redwoods set aside by California. This was in 1902. Muir Woods National Monument, in a mountain valley just across the Golden Gate Bridge from San Francisco, was established in 1908 in tribute to John Muir. The area covers less than one square mile, but the grove is cathedral-like. Then there are other state parks and Redwood National Park. And so on up the coast.

Cathedrals are for prayer, worship, exaltation, or soul-searching, and so are redwood groves. The trees favor river valleys or canyons that open to the sea, bringing together earth, sky, and water. Standing in a redwood grove in a chill mist calls to mind my visit to the Cathedral of Notre Dame in Paris during the uncertain days of World War II. The great church was then unheated and damp, evoking a grayish mood, yet I knew that it would always be there and that the mood would change, and I felt uplifted.

Standing at the base of a redwood and craning to see the very top of the soaring trunk, I appreciate the glory of life. The tree has been growing on this site for a thousand years or more. The redwood is the tallest living thing on earth, commonly growing more than 200 feet high, and occasionally more than 300 feet. Like Notre Dame, it should always be there, for there is no biological reason why a redwood must ever die. The thick furrowed bark is virtually fireproof. If fire should breach the bark, the wood itself is so water-laden that it offers a poor fuel. The redwood is saturated with tannin, which gives it resistance to fungi, rot, and parasites. In fact, the redwood does not even need to spring from seed, since it comes up readily from stumps and roots of veteran trees.

When settlement reached the Pacific the redwoods covered almost 2 million acres. The pioneers found them to be somewhat like their cousins of the High Sierra, the *Sequoia gigantea*—the giant sequoias, or Big Trees. There are differences in form and substance, however. The giant sequoia is more massive than the redwood, though not as tall. The bark of the *gigantea* is a bright reddish brown, that of the coast redwood, *Sequoia sempervirens*, a dull chocolate or cinnamon brown. The egg-shaped cones of the *sempervirens* are scarcely an inch long, only one-half the size, or even less, of the *gigantea* cones.

Then there's the question of the wood. The giant sequoias yield a brittle wood—not very good as lumber. The loss in felling is so great and the logs so difficult to handle that it is now practically off the market. The redwood is another story. The heartwood is straight grained, strong, and easy to work; it takes paint well and resists shrinkage, rot, and decay. "As lumber," said Muir, "the coast redwoods were too good to live."

Traveling up the coast, one finds little redwood forest in evidence. Most of the original 2-million-acre forest has been cut down and moved out. Now only about 10 percent remains. The rest of the forest has been scattered across America in railroad ties, bridge timbers, silos, posts, stakes, shingles, sidings, ceilings, doors, furniture, and caskets. The logging began only a little more than a century ago, quite logically along the banks bearing the most accessible—and stateliest—trees, so that I, and my generation, could hardly know the real magnificence of the redwoods.

The first successful effort at preservation came in 1902 when the Sempervirens Club saved the Big Basin, containing some of the largest remaining trees in the southern redwood belt, as a state park. The Save-the-Redwoods League, formed in 1918, set its sights on establishing a redwood national park, but then lowered them to merely raising funds to purchase primeval redwood forests for the California State Park System.

In the early 1960s only 2½ percent of the original redwood forests was protected in state parks. Until then it had been expected that

RHODODENDRON BLOOMS

landowners, including large timber companies, would ultimately sell to the state, since most of the remaining trees were on steep slopes difficult to reach and formed of shallow unstable soils that should never be logged. But with new machinery and techniques the great trees fell faster and faster. The scenic Redwood Highway was expanded into a freeway for logging trucks through the "saved" Humboldt Redwoods State Park. Companies spoke of the blessings of "scientific forestry" and "tree farming," but the logged-over areas failed to absorb heavy rains. Torrents of water and gravel runoff in disastrous floods toppled big trees downstream.

Meanwhile, in an area along Redwood Creek, researchers discovered a concentration of the tallest known living trees—with one giant reaching 367.4 feet above the ground—all on private land. This stimulated a movement for accelerated acquisition and once again for a national park. The most ambitious plan for a park, one of about 97,000 acres, was proposed by the Sierra Club. The timber industry fought the whole idea so ferociously

that only a compromise was possible. And when there's little left, how much can be saved with a compromise?

Redwood National Park, as established in 1968, would have preserved only a little more than 62,000 acres in fragmented units. Lands already publicly held in three state parks—Jedediah Smith Redwoods, Del Norte Coast Redwoods, and Prairie Creek Redwoods—made up almost half of the national park; the remainder was composed of formerly private lands, mostly redwood groves but also coastal bluffs and beaches. More of the primeval forest was left out of the park than was taken in, but fortunately this would later be rectified.

In August 1969, ceremonies were conducted to dedicate Lady Bird Grove, a stand of towering redwoods near the small town of Orick, 330 miles north of San Francisco. President Richard M. Nixon was present, along with Mrs. Lyndon B. (Lady Bird) Johnson and the evangelist Billy Graham, and all the right words were said. National recognition and—it was thought—protection had come at last to one of the natural wonders of the world.

There are beauty spots throughout the park, which ranges in elevation from 1,500 feet to sea level and includes 40 continuous miles of Pacific coastline. The western slopes drop off abruptly at the wild shores of Gold Bluffs, an area of sand flecked with gold, rugged promontories, and huge waves breaking over rocky shoals—definitely for watching and dreaming, rather than swimming and surfing.

The redwood forests in the state parks evoke a thousand moods of life old and new. North of Gold Bluffs Beach, Prairie Creek is almost a rain forest, with up to 100 inches of rain a year. Enough sunlight filters through the somber setting to make it a luxuriant botanical garden. Mosses and lichens cover the 50-foot-high walls of Fern Canyon. Coastal redwoods grow in company with Douglas fir, big-leaf maple, tanbark oak, and madrona. The last named is a beautiful broadleaf evergreen; its bright orange bark and shiny leaves make it seem, as Muir wrote, "like some lost wanderer from the magnolia groves of the South." In Prairie Creek park, a herd of about

200 tawny-colored Roosevelt elk roam free.

Del Norte contains four groves of redwoods, with steep slopes bearing the trees almost to the tide pools of the ocean shore. This is one of the rare places where the natural ecological transition from virgin redwood growth to a wild shoreline remains essentially undisturbed. Jedediah Smith, at the northernmost end of the national park, is at the eastern edge of the narrow redwood belt; thus it contains a mixture of coastal and inland trees, including ponderosa pine, along with a lush understory of rhododendron, azalea, fern oxalis, salal, and huckleberry. The redwood groves along Mill Creek are my favorites.

The world's tallest trees, however, are in the Emerald Mile along Redwood Creek, a region of rich, moist alluvial soil, lingering fog, and deep shadows. The tallest tree, as I mentioned, is 367.4 feet, while others rise above 350 feet. I often think that all national parks are incomplete at best, but nowhere else do I find such vivid evidence as at Redwood Creek. The passing of time demonstrated that these trees were inadequately protected by the 1968 park boundaries as other trees on steep facing slopes and the ridgetop outside the park were subjected to intensive logging. The resulting accelerated erosion turned Redwood Creek into a river running with rock and topsoil, raising fears during the 1970s that the tallest trees would not last much longer before being undermined and toppled.

In 1978 Congress voted to expand the park by 48,000 acres and to rehabilitate the watershed and cutover lands. It will be a long time before this work is done, and some of the finest stands have already been destroyed. They could have been preserved if the boundaries had been more adequately defined when the park was established; and the cost, in terms of dollars, would have been much lower.

At least now, within the 106,000 acres of this national park, the slender remnants of the once-vast Redwood Empire appear to be saved. Redwoods are long-lived trees, as the word *sempervirens* implies. I have walked among these trees, older by far than the white man's work on this continent, older than Notre Dame and other human masterworks in Europe, knowing that future generations will be able to derive the same inspiration from them.

DEL NORTE COAST

Yosemite National Park

THE INDIANS ARE NOW GONE, THOUGH THEY DWELLED IN YOSEMITE FOR CENTURIES. *Yosemite* is an Anglicized version of the tribe's name, also believed to be the Indians' term for "grizzly bear." And it's all that's left of either Indian or grizzly, of course. The Indians were still there in early 1851 when a military unit named the Mariposa Battalion arrived, soon after the Gold Rush had attracted inquisitive prospectors to the nearby foothills. The troops were on a punitive expedition. They evicted the Indians for daring to defend their territory and themselves against the miners. The gold booty, however, lay elsewhere.

Treasure other than gold was discovered at Yosemite. In 1855 James M. Hutchings, publisher of *California Magazine*, organized the first party of sightseers to enter Yosemite Valley; he followed up by publishing a series of glowing accounts complete with illustrations. Presently hotels were opened and toll roads built. Reaching Yosemite involved a rugged, dusty, bone-shattering trip by stage and saddle horse, yet Californians were determined to see this wonder of wonders in their midst.

Once the wagon roads were built, the influx really began. There was great competition among travel agencies in San Francisco, 150 miles away. Within ten years the Valley was well established as a tourist attraction; it was a thriving resort when Yellowstone was still an unknown wilderness. Horace Greeley came out from the East in 1859 and was overwhelmed by its grandeur. In a dispatch to the *New York Tribune*, he hailed Yosemite as "the greatest marvel of the continent." The strong tide of public interest led to Congressional passage of an act granting Yosemite Valley and the Mariposa Grove of Big Trees to California as a state park to be held "inalienable for all time"—a device to keep it safe from the claims of homesteaders and swindlers. President Abraham Lincoln signed the bill in June, 1864. These portions of Yosemite thus were established as America's first state park.

The most historic event in Yosemite (outside of its natural history) was John Muir's first trip to the park in 1868. Muir was wedded to and sired national parks, if this can be said of any man, but he bedded most often in Yosemite. Born in Scotland and raised in Wisconsin, he wanted nothing of cities, crowds, and merchandising. Though he traveled over a wide range of the West, including Alaska (and across the Bering Sea to Siberia), Muir's special kingdom was Yosemite. He lived there for six years among the ice-carved peaks and the immense domes, forming and proving his theory of glacial erosion.

HALF DOME

Muir was much like Henry David Thoreau —self-reliant, unflinching, loving of all life, basing standards of civilization on natural law. Thoreau once said: "I would that our farmers when they cut down a forest felt some of that awe which the old Romans did when they came to thin, or let in the light to, a consecrated grove, that is, would believe that it is sacred to some god.' In Muir's words: "One is constantly reminded of the infinite lavishness and fertility of Nature—inexhaustible abundance amid what seems enormous waste. And yet when we look into any of her operations that lie within reach of our minds, we learn that no particle of her material is wasted or worn out. It is eternally flowing from use to use, from beauty to higher beauty."

The establishment of Yosemite as a national park was largely due to Muir's persistent efforts. He was in great demand as a writer. More at home outdoors than indoors, he described the mountains in rare terms of poetry and science. In collaboration with Robert Underwood Johnson, his friend and editor at *Century Magazine*, Muir conducted a tireless campaign to make a national park of the Sierra peaks and slopes surrounding Yosemite Valley. They and their supporters achieved success in 1890. Sixteen years later, in 1906, California re-ceded the Valley and Mariposa Grove to the federal government for inclusion in the park.

Standing on the floor of Yosemite Valley, a region protected for over 100 years—albeit imperfectly at times—I sense Muir's living influence. He perceived the landscape as follows: "Vapor from the sea; snow and ice on the summits; glaciers and rivers—these form a wheel that grinds the mountains thin and sharp, sculptures deeply the flanks, and furrows them into ridge and canyon, and crushes the rocks into soils on which the forests and meadows and gardens and fruitful vine and tree and grain are growing."

From the floor of this profound gorge I begin to appreciate its dimensions. Yosemite Valley is one mile wide and seven miles long, carpeted with meadows and forests beside the clear waters of the Merced River. I look up at granite walls rising 2,000 to 4,000 feet, sheer in some places and cleft again by side canyons. El Capitan, the largest known single block of granite in the world, a geological wonder with scarcely a fracture in its entire perpendicular wall, stands guard at the lower end of the Valley. The massive proportions of El Capitan, Half Dome (the mythical Indian turned to stone), Glacier Point, Three Brothers, and the other domes and pinnacles are softened by shadows and by the green conifers growing beneath them.

Waterfalls too reflect the influence of rock structure on scenery. Yosemite's spectacular free-leaping waterfalls plunge from towering hanging valleys as though from some lost world. From a distance the falls look like strands of silver. At close range they sound like roaring volcanoes, perhaps like cannon fire. The waterfalls are noted for their height: Upper Yosemite Fall tumbles 1,430 feet over the north wall—a height equal to nine Niagaras. The Lower Yosemite Fall, immediately below, adds a drop of two more Niagaras. Counting the series of cascades in between, the combined distance measures 2,425 feet, making Yosemite Falls one of the highest waterfalls on earth, certainly the highest on this continent. Then there are Ribbon Fall, highest in terms of a single drop (1,612 feet sheer); lovely Bridalveil Fall, exploding in clouds of mist when it strikes the base; Nevada, Vernal, and Illilouette falls—all of them combining into a water spectacle that I doubt can be matched anywhere in the world.

The great falls are at their most thunderous from April to June, when winter snows are melting. They are still full early in July, but then decrease rapidly in volume. In late July much of the water reaches the base of Upper Yosemite Fall in the form of mist, projecting a lovely filmy grandeur.

Aspects of the whole Valley and its environs change with the seasons. When the falls are at their fullest and the Merced River is running high, mariposa lilies and other wild flowers spread carpets of color across the lower meadows. By July the upper meadows are bright with flowers. In early autumn many of the falls have practically disappeared, but in this season I can hike up to Glacier Point to overlook the changing colors of the oaks and the willow and cottonwood thickets across the Valley, and from there continue out to Sentinel Dome for an unobstructed panorama of the whole southern half of the park, ranging from San Joaquin Valley on the west to the wintry snowcapped ridge of the Sierra on the east. Here too, at Sentinel Dome, I can revisit the celebrated Jeffrey pine; stunted, gnarled, lightning-scarred, it draws its scant sustenance from cracks in the granite. "Scrawny little *Pinus jeffreyi,* whatever are you doing here," I would like to inquire, "when your brethren elsewhere are scarcely less magnificent in size than your cousins, *Pinus ponderosa*?" But the tree would likely reply, if it could, "None of your business!"

When is the weather here best? Best for what? Once, while tramping with my son when he was small, I complained about the awful weather. "It's not really awful," he corrected, "it's just raining." In November, the first storms over Yosemite Valley are relatively light. "The grand winter storms seldom set in before the end of November," Muir wrote. "The fertile clouds, descending, glide about and hover in brooding silence, as if thoughtfully examining the forests and streams with reference to the work before them; then small flakes or single crystals appear, glinting and swirling in zigzags and spirals; and soon the thronging feathery masses fill the sky and make darkness like night."

It was the glaciers that gouged Yosemite Valley into a U-shaped trough and sheared away the face of Half Dome. That took place long after the geologic ages during which a shallow sea spread inland from the Pacific across this whole area, long after the formation of a great block of the earth's crust some 400 miles long and from 50 to 80 miles wide that is now known as the Sierra Nevada, and long after streams flowing down the west front with torrential force cut deep canyons into the granitic rock. During the Ice Age, glaciers formed at the crest of the range and then followed the streams. The first of at least three glaciers extended down the Merced River as far as El Portal. During its farthest advance, the ice came within 700 feet of the top of Half Dome. The glaciers deepened Yosemite Valley 500 feet at the lower end and 1,500 feet opposite Glacier Point, then widened it by 1,000 feet at the lower end and 3,600 feet in the

EL CAPITAN AND MERCED RIVER >

upper half. The ice transformed the V-shaped stream-cut canyon into the sheer-walled U-shaped Valley for which the park is famous. The last glacier left a moraine of rock debris damming the Merced and forming a lake back into the Valley. Sediments that subsequently filled the lake form the level Valley floor today.

Glacial action rounded and polished domes like Liberty Cap in Little Yosemite Valley and Lembert Dome in Tuolumne Meadows. However, other domes, including Sentinel and Half Dome, are the result of exfoliation, a steady weathering, chipping, and crumbling of rock layers into rounded contours on their way to ultimate dissolution.

Such are the natural processes manifest in Yosemite. The national park is far larger and more beautiful than most people realize; the Valley is only a small part of it, though it is the best-known and most-loved part. Once there was another valley which many have said compared in beauty with Yosemite itself. Named Hetch Hetchy, it was located on the Tuolumne River beneath towering Hetch Hetchy Dome, LeConte Point, and Smith Peak. As early as 1882 city engineers of San Francisco scouted the possibility of damming Hetch Hetchy's narrow lower end to make a reservoir for water storage. The establishment of the national park in 1890, with Hetch Hetchy well within its boundaries, appeared to head that off, but the issue was pressed for years and never allowed to rest or die. Muir knew every part of Hetch Hetchy. "These sacred mountain temples are the holiest ground that the heart of man has consecrated," he wrote, "and it behooves us all faithfully to do our part in seeing that our wild mountain parks are passed on unspoiled to those who come after us, for they are national properties to which every man has a right and interest." Muir conceded the need of an adequate water supply, but he insisted it could be secured without disrupting the national park. Though it became a major national conservation battle, the fight to save Hetch Hetchy was lost in Congress in 1913, and the dam was built. Today, when Yosemite Valley is jammed and thousands are turned away for want of room, the flooding of Hetch Hetchy demands attention as a calamitous loss.

Five of the seven continental life zones are represented in Yosemite. They range from the Upper Sonoran in the warm foothills below Arch Rock at the El Portal entrance, 2,000 feet above sea level, to the Arctic-Alpine directly across the park at the windy summit of Mount Lyell, 13,114 feet high, on the eastern crest of the Sierra. Mount Lyell itself stands like a mighty wall of glistening granite above

a rampart of bright peaks in the Cathedral Range, flanked by Mount Maclure, just above 13,000 feet, and Rodgers Peak, a few feet below it. Hundreds of icy streams flow west from perpetual snowbanks through snow-bordered lakes, then tumble down from rocky heights to water luxuriant meadows. Lovely Tuolumne Meadows at the subalpine level, 8,600 feet, is the start of the John Muir Trail, extending south along the Sierra crest to Mount Whitney in Sequoia National Park.

The forests of Yosemite change as the Sierra rises. I follow them upward from the steep, hot canyons, where Digger pines give no shade in summer, into cool groves of bay trees, oaks, and pines and the groves of aspen that turn gold in autumn and from these to mountain junipers clinging to glacier-polished slopes—through one forest succeeding another until at last there is no forest, only the hardy marmots whistling shrilly in the rocks above timberline.

Which tree is the rarest, the most magnificent? Perhaps the sugar pine, king of all pines, towering upwards of 200 feet, its great branches sweeping outward and downward in graceful curves, the highest of them weighted by the largest cones I ever expect to see. Or perhaps the giant sequoias, those massive wonders that somehow escaped the glaciers of the Ice Age. Yosemite has three major groves of *Sequoia gigantea*, with the largest, the Mariposa Grove, containing more than 200 trees at least ten feet in diameter, surrounded by thousands of young trees looking upward to their future.

GLACIAL REMAINS ON YOSEMITE VALLEY FLOOR

Sequoia & Kings Canyon National Parks

THE SIERRA NEVADA, JOHN MUIR'S "RANGE OF LIGHT," IS THE COUNTRY'S HIGHEST MOUNTAIN range this side of Alaska; it is almost as massive as the Alps of France, Switzerland, and Italy combined. Rising gradually from the floor of the Central Valley on the west side, it ascends through 60 to 90 miles of foothills to a jagged crest from 7,000 to more than 14,000 feet in altitude, then plunges down a mile to the desertlike Great Basin on the east side. The range extends from the Cascades southward for some 400 miles, but I would say the heart of the Sierra lies within Sequoia and Kings Canyon national parks. The two parks are joined end to end and stretch 65 miles from north to south, protecting an unbroken wilderness of granite peaks, gorges, rockbound glacial lakes, flowering alpine meadows, and virgin forests. They are virtually a single unit, with Kings Canyon at the north, and are so administered. Within their boundaries the lofty Sierra reaches its climax in the 14,495-foot summit of Mount Whitney, the highest point in the United States south of Alaska.

It was the Spaniards who named the gallery of mountains that forms California's high backbone. Their romantic words for it, *Sierra Nevada*, mean "snow-covered mountain range." Everywhere within the more than 1,300 square miles of Sequoia and Kings Canyon I find excitement: in the colors of the range—white at dawn, golden at dusk, and, of course, white in winter (though I have never seen it then); in the vistas—viewed from the summit of the great monolith called Moro Rock—of both ridges of the Sierra's backbone at the horizon and of the silvery Kaweah River 4,000 feet below and almost straight down; in nine-mile-long Kings Canyon, plunging more than 8,000 feet from mountaintop to the bed of the South Fork of the Kings River, which the Spaniards called *Rio de los Santos Reyes* ("River of the Holy Kings"); and in the dense groves of imposing giant sequoias, the largest among these more than 3,000 years old and weighing well over a thousand tons.

Geologists say the Sierra Nevada may be 50 million years old, a block of the earth's crust uplifted and tilted in several stages, a fault-block range like the Tetons in Wyoming. Throughout the ice ages, U-shaped canyons were quarried, deep and wide. The glaciers polished canyon walls and high valleys and scooped out basins to be occupied by hundreds of lakes. Natural amphitheaters called "cirques" were gouged into ridges and crests. Thus the parks are filled with spectacular features. Of all the granite domes of the Sierra,

KINGS CANYON

Tehipite Dome, rising like a granite finger some 3,600 feet above the floor of Tehipite Valley, may be the most striking of all. Certainly Tehipite and Moro Rock compare with El Capitan and Half Dome in Yosemite.

It was not because of these geologic wonders, however, that the parks were established; the original legislation for both parks was designed to protect the Big Trees and nothing else. Sequoia is the second oldest national park, second only to Yellowstone. Established in 1890, five days before Yosemite, Sequoia encompasses the Giant Forest, including the largest tree—in terms of bulk—on earth. The smaller General Grant Grove, containing several of the very largest trees, was set aside in

the Yosemite Act as part of the General Grant National Park. Fifty years later, in 1940, after a struggle against power and irrigation interests, lumbermen, ranchers, stockmen, and hunters, Kings Canyon National Park was established. The new park included General Grant National Park and also embraced Tehipite Valley and majestic Kings Canyon, which had long been eyed for reservoir sites.

The General Sherman Tree, which is at least 3,500 years old, stands on guard at the entrance to the finest part of the Giant Forest, largest of the Big Tree groves. The tree was discovered in 1879 by trapper James Wolverton, companion of the legendary Hale Tharp, who was a pioneer cattleman in San Joaquin

Valley. Tharp was the first white man to see the Giant Forest. The General Sherman Tree is more than 272 feet tall and over 36 feet in diameter at its base. Wolverton named it after his commanding officer in the Civil War.

The General Grant Grove is one of America's most enchanting places. The General Grant Tree, from which it takes its name, measures 267 feet in height and 40 feet in diameter. The General Lee Tree in the same grove is almost as large. Though they are a few feet shorter than the General Sherman Tree, both are 100 feet higher than Niagara Falls. They have withstood the ravages of wind, storm, fire, and lightning for three millennia.

I look closely at the trees in the Giant Forest, the General Grant and other groves. They range in all sizes from tiny saplings to fallen giants toppled at last by some wintry blast, lying with roots uptorn. Each tree bespeaks its individuality, purpose, and unique characteristics, presenting some new phase of size, persistence, or growth. I think of the words of John Muir, in the midst of his "giants grouped in pure temple groves." He called the sequoia "king of all the conifers of the world, the noblest of a noble race." His veneration derived perhaps from his belief that the Indians drank the sap in hope of gaining some mystical power; he himself used rosy purple drops of sequoia sap in writing letters. I find the reddish-brown bark engrossing. Vertical breaks extending the length of the trunk give it a fluted appearance. The bark alone, spongy in substance, is often two feet thick, providing the tree protection against fire and insects. Tenacity of life and resistance to destruction make the sequoia a giant on earth, yet it grows from seeds that measure less than a centimeter.

The trees of the *Sequoia* group are survivors of an ancient race that flourished during Tertiary and Cretaceous times. They were as abundant as the pines are today, extending even into the Arctic Zone. Exactly why they almost vanished is not known. Apparently the glaciers swept away all but a few stands; most of the sequoias disappeared along with the mighty reptiles of a moist warm age.

The sequoia is now found in many distant parts, since seedlings have been successfully grown in nurseries and transplanted extensively in the eastern United States, the British Isles, and Central Europe. The giant sequoia, however, grows only in about 70 scattered groves on the western slopes of the Sierra Nevada in central California, at elevations from 4,000 to 8,000 feet. Its close relative, the coast redwood, grows near the Pacific Ocean in a narrow belt from Monterey to southern Oregon. The coast redwood is the

GENERAL GRANT TREE,
KINGS CANYON NATIONAL PARK

world's tallest tree, rising on a slender trunk, whereas the giant sequoia is the world's largest tree in volume, its immense trunk rising without the taper that is characteristic of most trees. Its limbs are heavier and more angular than the redwood's, its seeds and cones at least twice as large.

It would be a rich experience to observe the General Grant Grove or the Giant Forest, Cedar Grove or the Redwood Mountain Grove, in every season of the year. In winter, when deep snow accumulates, the Big Trees are draped with snowy candelabra that contrast with their somber summer dress. Before winter is over, tiny bright yellow flowers burst forth from the limbs in a golden spray. Sequoias seldom grow in pure stands: generally the forest floor is covered with flowering shrubs and trees, including lupine, redbud, laurel, and dogwood, creating spring and autumn contrasts of color and light in dark groves. The sequoias tower as patriarchs among a forest of incense cedar, white fir, Douglas fir, ponderosa pine, or the sugar pine —a majestic tree in its own right—a complex of infinite life and fascination.

Extensive as the present groves in Sequoia and Kings Canyon parks appear to be, I can't avoid learning the painful lesson that they don't begin to match the forest of just one century ago. Big Stump Basin, in the southwest corner of the General Grant Grove, is filled with ghostly reminders of early logging. Between 1862 and 1900, logging operations decimated groves more glorious than anything now preserved. At the Centennial Stump I look at the remains of a huge tree that was cut up in sections and shipped to the Centennial Exposition in 1876. Further destruction took place when a sawmill was built about nine miles from the Giant Forest, as part of an illfated cooperative colony. Fortunately, Americans learned and acted in time to place values where they belong. The General Sherman Tree is said to contain enough wood to build about 40 homes of five rooms each. I daresay some Americans would cut it down—but I like to think only a few. The nation as a whole has decreed that the tree is worth more standing where it is, reaching as high as the Capitol dome in Washington and no less a treasure.

Tree-cutting was only one of the early threats. Even after Sequoia was established as a national park, pioneer settlers resisted government control. Hunters and trappers took unlimited numbers of bear, deer, and fur-bearing animals. Sheepmen drove huge flocks into the high mountain meadows, destroying grass and herbage. Muir complained bitterly, calling sheep "hoofed locusts." All this went on even while the Cavalry was in charge of the newly formed park. Muir recognized the fragile nature of the highlands. "A great portion of the woody plants that escape the feet and teeth of the sheep," he wrote in his book *The Mountains of California*, "are destroyed by the shepherds by means of running fires." The fires were set during the dry season to burn off underbrush and old tree trunks in order to improve the pasture, but they took young trees and seedlings as well, setting in motion a long train of evils.

Sequoia and Kings Canyon national parks have hundreds of miles of hiking and riding paths, including a stretch of the famous John Muir Trail, which runs 218 miles along the crest of the Sierra between Mount Whitney and Yosemite Valley. Every year, more and more hikers and backpackers are following these routes. The high country, with its granite domes and beautiful lakes, its alpine valleys and sparkling plunging streams, needs to be used lightly, even by those who love it—those who follow its trails in search of the atmosphere of the original California.

GIANT BOLES OF *SEQUOIA GIGANTEA*

GENERAL SHERMAN TREE, SEQUOIA NATIONAL PARK

Hawaii Volcanoes National Park

OW COULD I FORESEE THAT I WOULD COME TO MAUNA LOA TOO SOON, JUST A FEW months too soon? I had no way of knowing that in July, 1975, Mauna Loa, one of the largest volcanoes in the world, would signal its intentions with tremors in the earth, that it would erupt in a six-mile curtain of fire at the Mokuaweoweo Crater and a two-pronged lava flow from Pohaky Hanalei, that earthquakes would continue at the rate of one or two a minute as many as five days later. All I could do then was to wish I had been there on the island of Hawaii when Mauna Loa erupted.

Ever since man has watched them, Mauna Loa and Kilauea, its smaller sister in Hawaii Volcanoes National Park, have been active off and on with one volcanic eruption or another. Perhaps at some future time I may witness one of the big outbursts and then be able to report as James A. Michener did: "A group of us from Honolulu stayed at the rim all night, watching with fascination as the dark-red fires formed endless patterns on the crater floor, with now and then an explosion which sent rocks hurtling toward us. It was an unforgettable view of the world's interior forces at work."

Hawaii, the Big Island, almost twice as large as all the other islands in the chain combined, is the southernmost and the youngest, the last one formed of accumulated lava rising upward from the floor of the sea. Even now its young volcanoes grow with energy, keeping ahead of the agents of erosion.

The tallest volcanic peak, snow-covered Mauna Kea, rises 13,796 feet above sea level. When measured from its base on the ocean bottom, it is well over 30,000 feet high, making it the biggest mountain mass in the world. Though Mauna Kea has been quiet in historic times, the other volcanic peaks on the Big Island have not. The most spectacular eruption in Hawaii's recorded history occurred in 1959, when a line of lava fountains sprang from Kilauea Iki, the large pit just east of Kilauea Crater. One "fountain" grew until it was gushing molten lava, mixed with sulfurous steam, that rose to a fantastic height of 1,900 feet, destroying a campsite and many acres of the bordering Tree Fern Forest. But the very next year, 500 acres of new land were added to the island as lava spilled from the Puna rift zone into the sea.

Since my first flight to Hawaii 30 years ago, I have seen, from distances of more than 100 miles, Mauna Loa's great dome rising 13,680 feet above the sea, providing a welcome reassurance that land lies ahead. Mauna Loa's lava flows have covered more than half the island, accounting for over 2,000 square miles of its land area. Its 1949 eruption continued for almost five months. A year later it produced about one billion tons of lava. Then it slumbered for 25 years until the fireworks starting July 5, 1975.

In other parts of the world people flee when volcanoes erupt. In Hawaii the reverse takes place. At the first sign of a new eruption Hawaii's residents compete for ringside seats. Volcanoes here seem ferocious, but they are not of the explosive-reaction type emitting great clouds of ash. These gentle giants seldom become dangerous even while liberating fiery rivers of lava from vents and cracks. This is one of the reasons the volcanoes were incorporated in Hawaii National Park—along with Haleakala, on Maui—when it was established in 1916. (The park was renamed in 1960.)

At Kilauea, the most active volcano in the world, I can see where the summit, 4,090 feet above sea level, has collapsed to form a broad caldera. I look into Halemaumau ("House of Everlasting Fire"), the fire pit which the legendary volcano goddess Pele calls home. For many years the pit contained a lake of active, splashing lava, variously rising and overflowing, then sinking. At Thurston Lava Tube I explore a tunnel-like formation that was

PAHOEHOE LAVA

HALEMAUMAU FIRE PIT AND AMAUMAU FERN

strangely shaped when the outer crust of lava hardened and the inner portion flowed away.

Exotic trees and lovely flowers have emerged in this strange atmosphere. At the Tree Fern Forest I walk through a lush jungle blessed by northeast trade winds forcing moisture-laden clouds up the mountain slopes. Rains that average 100 inches annually sustain many varieties of ferns, overtowered by a dense growth of tropical ohia trees. And wherever the ohia blooms, the apapane appears. This small nectar-sucking bird is as red as the feathery ohia blossom, called "lehua," it feeds on, but its wings are black, its belly light gray. Equally abundant here are the amakihi, a small yellow-green insect gatherer, and the elepaio, a perky flycatcher.

I find one of the strangest areas at Kipuka Puaulu, the "Bird Park," an "island" of old surface surrounded by young lava flows. In the forested section are about 40 varieties of trees, some peculiar to this island, a few the only living representatives of their vanishing species. But on the fresh rock surfaces of the younger lava flows I see the pioneers of a new forest—the sturdy ohia, the colorful aalii, and the pukeawe shrubs.

There are nene, the Hawaiian geese, here too, as at Haleakala. I visit them in pens where they have lately arrived from captive breeding.

A park biologist explains that earlier some of them had been released at upper levels of 5,000 to 6,500 feet, the wild flock's final stronghold. Now the national park seeks to clean out feral goats and reestablish the nene at lower elevations, returning some of Hawaii's natural treasures to their original home.

Traces of an ancient culture are here also: petroglyphs along the coast, and the ruins of Wahaula Heiau, which may be the oldest temple in Hawaii, built by Paao, the powerful early Tahitian priest. It was he who introduced the severe system of taboos and sacrifices. In fact, this temple, twice rebuilt, served as one of the six sanctuaries where ruling chiefs prayed and where humans were slain to be offered in sacrifice to the gods. Paao's system of rites was practiced till as recently as 1819.

The ideas of the ancients perhaps were in tempo with the volcanoes. The forces from deep within the earth spewed molten rivers over the land, and these have taken as much as a century to cool. At Kau Desert I examine weird formations solidified in black, gray, and purple patterns, the barren lava, the wind-blown ash and pumice moving as dunes from crater rim to seacoast. Those early Polynesians worked a marvel in crossing the Pacific to Hawaii, but how could they ever cope with enigmatic volcanoes? For that matter, how can we, even now?

There is one vista in this park that I would rank among the most inspiring in national parks anywhere. From Hilina Pali, a fault-block cliff, I look down at the coast, 2,250 feet below. There lie the gleaming crystalline black sands of Punaluu Beach and beyond them Ka Lae, or South Cape, the southernmost point in the United States. This southeast coast, un-touched and unspoiled, reveals our earth still being formed, without really indicating what may be next.

NEW LAVA FLOW ON MAUNA LOA

KOA TREES ON MAUNA LOA TRAIL

Haleakala National Park

IN HALEAKALA NATIONAL PARK, ON MAUI IN THE HAWAIIAN ISLANDS, I ARRIVE AT THE RIM OF one of the largest volcanic craters on earth. I look down 3,000 feet to the 19-square-mile floor of the crater and focus on nothing else but the "House of the Sun." The crater's floor and walls are pitted with spattered cinder cones, lava flows, and volcanic rocks streaked with red, yellow, gray, and black. The tallest of these multicolored forms, Puu o Maui, rises more than a thousand feet above the floor, while the surface of the Bottomless Pit, a debris-choked old vent, is some 65 feet deep. It is an absolutely weird environment of strange plants, rare birds, and rock where nothing grows, but I believe this place has a quality that makes it as useful and valid as any productive forest or prairie.

Rising 10,023 feet above the Pacific Ocean, Haleakala is presently a dormant volcano. Its last eruptions, minor ones, occurred two centuries ago. Haleakala is living witness to land-forming volcanic explosions of the Pacific Ocean floor. Millions of years ago the earth's crust trembled and then cracked, as it is apt to do, but in this case the crack was 1,600 miles long and 18,000 feet below the surface of the ocean. Out of it came fiery volcanic actions continuing over long periods, with new sheets of lava building upon the old until finally they emerged above the waves to become the chain of islands called Hawaii.

The islands are the volcanic peaks of a mountain range greater under the water than above it. On Maui, the second-largest island, the volcanic head continued to grow while other portions of the island were being tempered into fertile fields. Then the great basin of Haleakala was molded by centuries of erosion, of wind and water, even as volcanic explosions continued.

I reached Haleakala by traveling up through an environment that seemed to me unreal, or misplaced, in Polynesia. Condominiums, shopping centers, hotels, highways,

SILVERSWORD

and crowds have preempted the tropic countryside, open beaches, and banyan trees. Only Haleakala is still worthy of the Polynesian legends. According to myth, the demigod Maui captured the sun and held it prisoner here in order to assure his people more daylight hours. I can accept the legend. I can understand Haleakala as a spiritual focus for the ancients—where food offerings would be left wrapped in ti leaves in sacred areas, where bones of what may be Hawaiian chiefs would be interred in a rugged lava bed high on the crater's slopes. Little wonder that Mark Twain came here and then rhapsodized about Haleakala in his classic, *Roughing It*. If all else went wrong, he once wrote in a letter, he would shut himself "in the healing solitudes of the crater of Haleakala and get a good rest." Today, where better on Maui?

I am not surprised to learn here that Haleakala supports rare birds—distinctly Hawaiian—such as the Maui nukupuu, a honeycreeper long thought extinct; the bright green and yellow amakihi, which pursues insects and nectar at top speed; the beautiful iiwi, with bright scarlet body, black wings and tail, and inch-long curved bill; and above all the Hawaiian goose, or nene.

The return of the nene from near extinction is a heartwarming story of human concern. It is called a "native bird," but no one knows how the nene first came to Hawaii. Its ancestors may have been Canadian geese swept from their migratory course by some violent storm to find haven in Hawaii's benign environment, where they adapted over thousands of years to climate and habitat far removed from Arctic tundra and marshy wetlands. Though the nene has entirely forsaken the water, its feet retain some webbing, now toughened to accommodate the sharp lava.

Once the nene were found in great flocks, but they were overtaken by one catastrophe after another. For a time they were hunted. Goats, introduced to the islands following the arrival of Captain James Cook in 1778, competed with the nene for habitat. The lowlands were planted in sugarcane and pineapple, depriving the birds of still more of their domain. Predatory mongooses were released to control rats and mice damaging the sugarcane, but they spread and "controlled" the nene as well. By the end of World War II less than 30 remained in the wild, and the native Hawaiian goose was considered virtually extinct.

In 1949 a program was begun to raise nene for release into the wild, based on several captive birds held by Herbert Shipman, a Hawaiian rancher. The captive stock has since been raised at Pohakuloa on the Big Island

of Hawaii and at distant Slimbridge, England, site of the famous Wildfowl Trust headed by Sir Peter Scott. The program has worked. More than 1,300 nene have been returned to the wild, in both Haleakala and Hawaii Volcanoes national parks and in other sanctuaries on state-owned and private lands.

I once saw a flock of nene in the civilized setting at Slimbridge. Can any of them be the same birds I meet feeding on the wild grasses, leafy plants, and berries near Paliku Cabin deep inside the northeast corner of Haleakala? Here they were released in 1962 in a rare lush haven amidst volcanic ash, a touch of verdant magic bred by clouds moving up the windward slopes and spilling over the rim.

The plants that grow among the cones, cinders, pumice, and ash of Haleakala are unusual too. They include the linchen, or Hawaiian snow, which is the first plant to appear following a lava flow at higher elevations, the sandalwood tree, and a host of shrubs with striking flowers or berries. The most unusual plant may be the yuccalike silversword. A rare relative of the sunflower, it is part tree, part flower, and part cactus. At one time it probably covered many acres of the crater floor, but those days are gone. Now I find the silversword at the Kalahaku Overlook in an area enclosed to protect the plants from roaming goats and thoughtless visitors. Its long narrow leaves gleam like frosted silver. After years of growth each plant produces one flower stalk, sometimes up to nine feet high, bearing a hundred or more small but vivid purplish blooms. Once the seeds of the bloom mature, the plant dies.

Although Haleakala has been protected since 1916 (first as part of Hawaii National Park), the Kipahulu District, including the Seven Pools, was added to the park in 1969. I reach this new portion via the Hana area, relatively isolated and less developed than other parts of Maui. Kipahulu and Hana are rich in Hawaiian legend and history, evidenced by remains of old taro patches, shelter sites, rock walls, and pictographs. This was the ancient battleground where chiefs of the island of Hawaii attempted to wrest control of Maui and where King Kamehameha I, who eventually conquered all of the islands, fought one of his early important battles. I find trees and plants brought by the Polynesians when they came here nearly 2,000 years ago—the kukui, milo, banana, breadfruit, hau, ti, and coconut. Kukui was important to the ancients, who burned its oil in torches.

The waters of the Seven Pools cascade in succession from one pool to another, the last emptying into the ocean. The pool at the top is formed in a deep gorge below a waterfall dropping 200 feet. Bordering the lower pools, the pandanus, or hala, looks like a palm, but its fruit resembles a pineapple.

The rain forest surrounding the Seven Pools is lush with native trees. This is beyond a doubt one of the most enchanting places on earth. In the graveyard of the little Congregational Church just beyond the park boundary, I find the burial plot of Charles A. Lindbergh, who returned to his home in Hana in 1974 to die and find his peace. He could not have chosen a resting place more symbolic of his own life and dreams.

< CINDER CONES AND SILVERSWORD   OVERLEAF: NORTH RIM OF GRAND CANYON >

THE SOUTHWEST

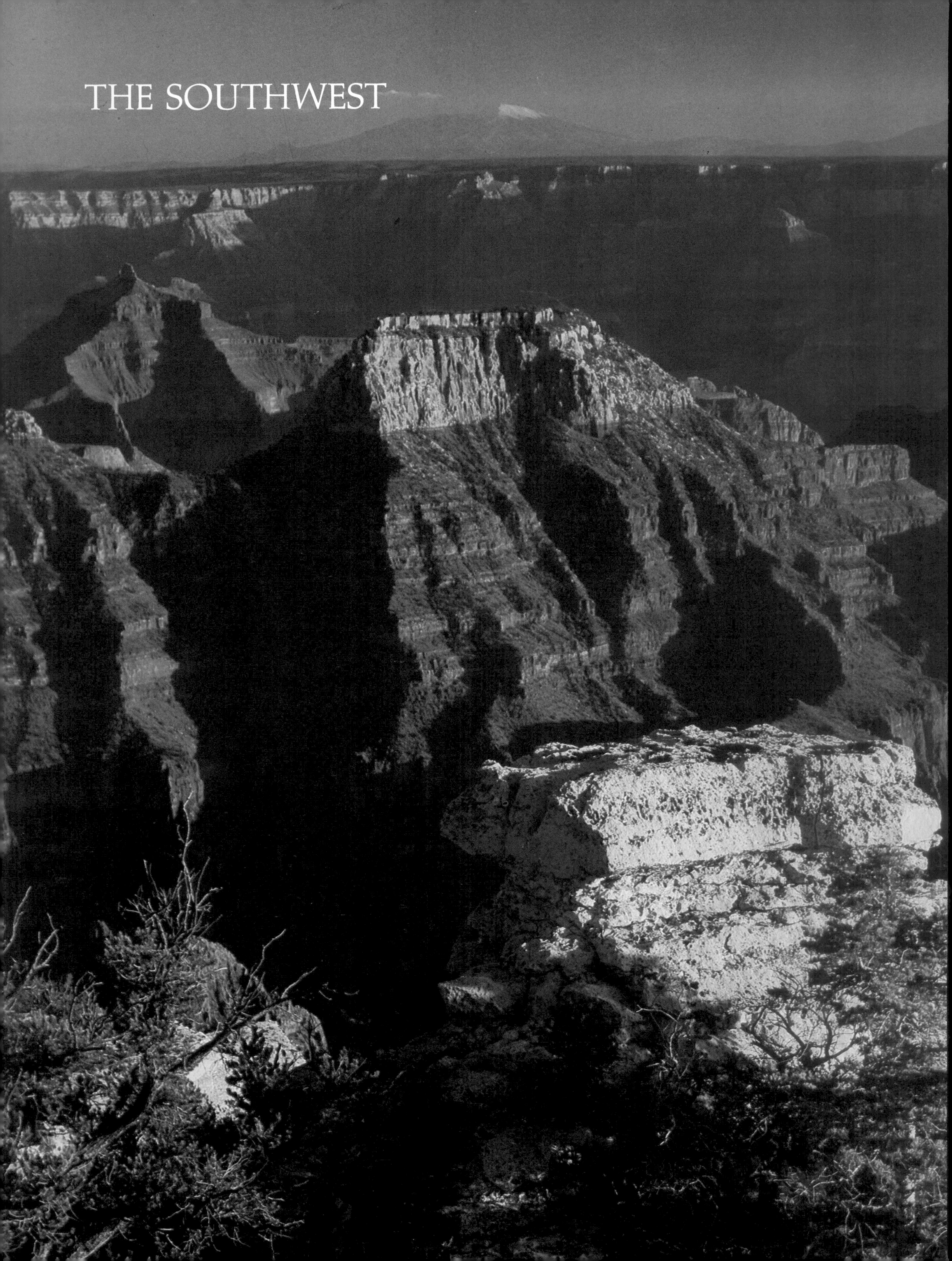

Grand Canyon National Park

THE GRAND CANYON IS MORE THAN A PLACE. IT'S ALSO A SYMBOL. IT SYMBOLIZES WHAT'S really right about America, a portion of the native land that somehow, somewhere is still free of corruption, pollution, the imprint of supertechnology. Freedom is an idea and dream about the rights of every human being, but the earth too must be accorded rights, if only to sustain those of the people who dwell on it. Thus the Grand Canyon is like the flag that must not fall. So long as this mighty chasm remains undefiled, the dream also remains valid.

I approach the Canyon through country full of the familiar, but when I reach the edge of the South Rim I feel humbled, cleansed of self-interest. The earth seems suddenly to have opened. Immensity is the first overwhelming impression, immensity of breadth and depth. In form, size, and flaming color, nothing in North America—nothing on earth, so far as I know—comes close to the giant bowl carved by the Colorado River in northwestern Arizona.

The open earth sinks down from the rim, through age by geological age, precipice to precipice, until it reaches the river, the straw-colored thread running through dark rocks formed in the earth's first cooling more than 2 billion years ago. Mountains and plateaus rise between South Rim and North Rim in the same shapes that men have used for building temples.

There is so much to the Grand Canyon that one could spend a lifetime of observation and learning and still end with a greater sense of wonder and with more questions unanswered than at the beginning. It takes time to see the Canyon properly, to feel it fully, to allow messages to filter through city-hardened defenses and touch the mind and inner spirit. Even simple viewing from the rim requires time—time to follow shadows crossing canyon walls and blue-hazed peaks, time to watch brilliant colors change. In soft morning light, for instance, blue, purple, and pastel hues seem to dominate. When clouds fill the overhead skies, colors go flat. On a clear afternoon, late sunlight illuminates the walls with a burst of golden light.

At the South Rim I am hardly alone. It's like a tourist village. For nearly a century tourists have converged here, responding to exhortations like Theodore Roosevelt's when he hailed the Grand Canyon as "the one great sight which every American should see." I stand next to a group that has arrived on the scenic flight package tour from Las Vegas which provides time for lunch, souvenir shopping, and a few minutes at the rim before returning to slot machines and gambling tables. Doubtless these people derive some pleasure from their brief interlude, but can it amount to much of meaning?

The Grand Canyon was not always this easy to reach. Until the turn of the century it took an expedition, or considerable daring, to penetrate the Canyon. The river itself was considered impossible to traverse; everyone was convinced it would never be run. As Lieutenant Joseph Christmas Ives wrote after traveling through the area in 1858: "It seems intended by nature that the Colorado River, along the greater portion of its lonely and majestic way, shall be forever unvisited and undisturbed."

Within a few years, however, the intrepid John Wesley Powell embarked on his wild classic adventure. Despite the loss of one arm at the Battle of Shiloh during the Civil War, Powell was an undaunted explorer. With nine companions he set out in 1869 on the first of his two scientific expeditions down the Green and Colorado rivers into Arizona; this was the only region trappers and traders in the era of Jim Bridger, Jedediah Smith, and the Sublettes had missed. The expedition saw wild country that few, if any, white men had seen before—treacherous canyons, a lonely land of isolated settlements, Indian shepherds, and hardy wild animals. Mishaps, near starvation, and the desertion of three men who climbed out of the canyons only to be slain by Indians, limited the scientific work, but Powell studied the canyon walls stratum by stratum and accumulated a wealth of data. The accounts of his hair-raising experiences appeared in his popular books, *First Through the Grand Canyon*, *Explorations of the Colorado River and Its Tributaries*, and *Canyons of the Colorado*.

Perhaps anyone who visits the Grand Canyon, for no matter how short a stay, should be required to read these books first. "Past these towering monuments, past these mounded billows of orange sandstone, past these oak-set glens, past these fern-decked alcoves, past these mural curves," Powell

CANYON BELOW UPSET RAPIDS

56

VIEW THROUGH GRAND CANYON ARCH

wrote, "we glide hour after hour, stopping now and then as our attention is arrested by some new wonder."

I head into the Canyon on the steep switchbacks of Bright Angel Trail. Once it was used by Indians to gain access to a cottonwood oasis 3,100 feet below the rim. Now it's well trodden by an endless stream of hikers and mule riders. At the edge of the trail a variety of plants grow wherever there is soil among the rocks for a root to dig into. Among them I note gilia, penstemon, and paintbrush. The Grand Canyon is scarcely described as a botanical wonderland, though it well might be, considering the tremendous range in elevation and soil settings.

The North and South rims are only nine miles apart, as the crow flies, but their environments are distinctly different. The North Rim averages 1,200 feet higher. It is heavily grown with ponderosa pine, quaking aspen, lovely blue spruce, and flowering mountain meadows characteristic of the cool, moist Kaibab Plateau. The South Rim, 7,000 feet above sea level, is more typical of the arid land, with a cover of pinyon and juniper. And then there's the hot, dry desert of the Inner Gorge, like southern Arizona or Mexico, except, of course, for lush growth around the river and springs.

White-throated swifts swish jetlike close to the cliffs, heralding a mule string plodding the familiar course to Phantom Ranch at the base of the Canyon. I remember the clop-clop and snort of the mule in Ferde Grofe's *Grand Canyon Suite* that made it seem so adventurous and beyond reach.

Out across the Canyon the rock layers exposed to view are pages in the textbook of earth's history. The layers include gray Kaibab limestone walls, formed with shells, corals, and sponges of a long-forgotten sea; buff-colored Coconino sandstone, the solidified remains of sand dunes where ancient lizards have left their footprints; red and green shales, with traces of primitive cone-bearing plants and fossil ferns—layer upon layer until finally millions of years have been spanned in a day, or in less than a mile down.

At Indian Garden I stop for water and to rest in the shade where native Havasupai once irrigated farm plots from natural springs. Despite the seeming hostility of the area, even the land below the rims supported prehistoric people in family-size cliff dwellings, farming small gardens and feeding on edible greens and fruits around them. The temperature rises with descent into the inner gorge, and with it the vegetation changes. The century plant, an agave, grows on rocky slopes in company with narrow-leaf yucca. Mesquite, creosote, and a variety of cacti spread over limestone soils and rock. Jumping cholla is one I know well enough to diligently avoid, having once been stuck painfully by its spiny needles, and then found them tough to remove.

Beyond the narrow Kaibab Suspension Bridge, the only crossing of the Colorado River in the national park, I arrive at Bright Angel Campground, across the creek from Phantom Ranch, only a mile down but an eight-mile trip from my starting point at the South Rim. Here the river is a living, roaring presence, though it seems more mud than water. "Too thick to drink and too thin to plow," said old-timers of the endless sediment it bears, more than a half million tons of it every day. Plainly the Grand Canyon is still abuilding, widening and deepening. Century after century its walls have weathered, crumbled, and tumbled shreds of sand, gravel, mud, and rock into the water, giving the river new tools for scouring and gouging. Daylight is short between the high, dark Canyon walls at the base. Descending is the easier part by far. Climbing out is something else.

Navajo and Hopi live east of the national park. Hualapai and Paiute are neighbors too. The Havasupai live in a portion of the park once hidden and remote, which their fathers have occupied for more than 800 years. Hundreds of ruins throughout the park bespeak even earlier dwellers.

From Hualapai Hilltop I ride a packhorse down the precipitous switchback trail to the home of the Havasupai, the "lost village of the Grand Canyon," only to find it isn't really all that lost. The Havasupai live 70 miles from the nearest town by road, then another eight miles down the tortuous trail. Until recently there was almost no change in their life-style, which revolved around basketmaking, enough agriculture to feed themselves, and crude, dilapidated dwellings. They still derive much of their livelihood from livestock and irrigated fields along the canyon floor. But tourism is their main industry. Tourists fly in by helicopter, some to stay overnight at the campground or tourist lodge, others less than an hour on quickie excursions. It doesn't sound quite the way to visit "the most isolated Indian tribe in the United States."

Havasupai Canyon I find to be actually a narrow side canyon, barely a mile at its widest, off the main canyon. Havasupai Creek, the main stream, is fed by underground springs which send clear, fresh water cascading down four major waterfalls into pools and through scores of lesser drops in its ten-mile rush to join the muddy Colorado.

Copper-skinned children with huge brown eyes frolic in the blue-green waters, ignoring the tourists except to demonstrate that they can always go swimming when it's hot. The creek gives life and beauty to the banks as well, nourishing giant willows and cottonwoods that provide shade and coolness in contrast with the stark desert of the upper plateau. Ferns and moss cling to weirdly draped travertine deposits built up beside the falls.

Long ago the Indians set up irrigation ditches to channel water to patches where they raise grain, fruit, and vegetables. Gardens grow in the backyards while horses graze the

FOG-SHROUDED CANYON FROM MATHER POINT

front. The village has a population of 400. Young Havasupai leave to try their hand elsewhere, but keep returning, despite frustration, to live by the blue-green water.

When I glance up at the Grand Wash Cliffs from the ranger patrol boat on the river, they appear to be a high, broken vertical wall. On approaching closer, I can see the cliffs defined as a series of bold steplike slopes displaying a wealth of color. The Grand Wash Cliffs mark the western end of the high plateaus through which the Colorado River has carved the wonder called the Grand Canyon.

For almost 300 miles the Colorado River still flows free—from Lees Ferry just below Glen Canyon Dam to the Grand Wash Cliffs. For millions of years the water of the river and its tributaries has been carving the Canyon; this water, in fact, is a vital factor in the future of the Grand Canyon as a natural feature. But change has been coming on, imprinting civilization on the wild country and continually influencing the flow of the river.

First came Hoover Dam, creating a reservoir 115 miles long called Lake Mead, from which the ranger and I have come past the Grand Wash Cliffs into Lower Granite Gorge. Then at the eastern end of the Grand Canyon came Glen Canyon Dam and Lake Powell, opening access by powerboat to remote places such as Rainbow Bridge, the largest known natural stone arch, and Hole-in-the-Rocks, where a Mormon party made a daring, seemingly impossible crossing of the Colorado with hundreds of cows and sheep and 80 wagons.

More recently came the huge power plant at Page, adjacent to Glen Canyon Dam, part of the massive coal-fired, steam, and electricity

generation and transmission system emerging in the Four Corners region of the Southwest. Plans to construct the giant Kaiparowits plant have been withdrawn, but completion of the remainder of this network would irrevocably disrupt the character of the land, and more than half of all the American Indians now living on reservations would be subject to air pollution. Hundreds of Navajo already have been displaced from the high plateau known as Black Mesa to make way for stripmining of their coal resources. The Hopi, who have lived in harmony with their environment for seven centuries, will be hit the hardest. Few in number, they stand in the way of the demands of supercities.

So does Grand Canyon National Park stand in the way of these demands. The Grand Canyon had been a national monument until 1919, when it was designated a national park. To protect it from construction of new dams, Congress enlarged the park in 1975 to encompass the river from below Glen Canyon Dam to the Grand Wash Cliffs. But there is *still* pressure for another dam, park or no park.

From the river I view the Music Mountains and the Hualapai Indian Reservation, presenting a jumble of gorges, cliffs, and inaccessible mesas. Much of this rugged land is heavily grazed by domestic livestock, yet it's still known to include at least 300 different plant species and to provide sanctuary for such rare wildlife forms as mountain sheep and mountain lions. The Grand Canyon is an endless composition of springs, seeps, caves, waterfalls and cascades as much as 1,000 feet high, and, of course, the flowing river. "Do nothing to mar its grandeur," said President Theodore Roosevelt after his first visit in 1903—a challenge for each generation to meet in turn.

< MOONEY FALLS, GRAND CANYON NATIONAL PARK

Zion National Park

THE MORMON PIONEERS WERE RIGHT WHEN THEY CHOSE ZION IN SOUTHWESTERN UTAH AS A retreat and special place of reverence, calling it the "heavenly city of God" and giving religious names to rock formations, which they saw as natural temples, cathedrals, altars, pulpits, and landings for angels.

Rocks, some of the most brilliantly colored on earth, are the principal feature of Zion National Park, "Land of the Rainbow Canyons." Yet I also appreciate the plants and trees that contrast and harmonize with the stone masses, especially considering that arid, variable climate and geologic forces have made it tough for anything to grow here. In Zion Canyon moisture comes mostly from sudden summer thundershowers, with some from winter snow; but summers generally are long, hot, and dry, so vegetation must prove itself hardy and adapt to the environment. The water-loving plants are something else, crowding the streambeds and growing in types of nooks and crannies found in few other places.

Passing through Springdale, an early Mormon settlement, I drive along the North Fork of the Virgin River into Zion Canyon, the heart of the park. One great monolith after another, blazing with color, lines the river's course. The name of the river is intriguing in itself, particularly since the Towers of the Virgin rise among the West Temple, the Altar of Sacrifice, the Beehives, and Sentinel Peak. However, towers and river are no kin; the latter has nothing to do with virgins. It was named by Jedediah Smith, the explorer and trapper, for his contemporary, Thomas Virgin (though I have never seen reference to this gentleman elsewhere).

The river has carved the curving gorge through walls of sandstones and shales that reveal a tempestuous past. Imbedded in the rocks are traces of life left from ancient oceans, marshes, and bayous where dinosaurs and other reptiles wallowed, from wide and swift-flowing rivers, from tropical lowlands with forests of tree ferns and cycads, from deserts and shifting sand dunes. The entire span of civilization as we know it seems hardly a second in the sweep of geological history of southern Utah. It's a humbling thought.

Zion National Park is part of a province called the Colorado Plateau, a rugged semiarid land of raised plains and basins spread over portions of Colorado, Arizona, Utah, and New Mexico, where eons of erosion—induced largely by the Colorado River and its tributaries—and weathering have peeled open the pages of earth. If I had lived earlier and held the authority, I might have designated *all* of

southern Utah as a national park, so rich and abundant are its natural values. A few key portions have been set aside, including Zion and Bryce Canyon national parks in the western section; Capitol Reef National Park in the central section; and Arches and Canyonlands national parks in the eastern section, plus several national monuments and small state parks. But in much of the area left unprotected, the character of the region has already been altered.

Ferns and flowers soften the floor of Zion Canyon. Cottonwood trees are prevalent, as they are throughout the West, taken for granted and rather unloved because they've always been there. Viewing and reviewing these trees convinces me they deserve better. In spring they produce many hair-covered seeds, giving the appearance of cotton, hence the name. In late autumn their firm-textured leaves turn to brilliant gold. Southern Utah pioneers used the ashes of the cottonwood as a source of lye, which they mixed with animal fats to make soap. Whether useful or not,

cottonwoods enrich the landscape. Old trees in particular take on a gnarled appearance worthy of portraiture.

Scrubby live oaks, with prickly hollylike leaves, spread in low thickets across the rocky, dry slopes. The live oak is not much loved either, though it provides valuable cover in slowing down the removal of soil that often accompanies summer thundershowers. And the live oak keeps its leaves all winter, which many other trees cannot do. Canyon wild grape I see in profusion on the floor of Zion Canyon and in the side canyons. Lacking sufficient self-support, this woody vine attaches itself to trees and makes canopies over shrubs. The grapes taste too sour to me, but the Indians ate them both fresh and dried, and the pioneers found them to be an excellent source of jelly. Even now birds eat the small, dark grapes, and mule deer consume the large, heart-shaped leaves and tender vine.

Among the many wild flowers growing on the canyon floor, none is more unusual than the "Zion moonflower," reaching heights of two feet or more, its summer-blooming large,

SANDSTONE RELIEF

61

TEMPLE OF SINAWAVA

white trumpet-shaped flowers opening in the evening and wilting beneath the morning sun. The evening primrose is another night bloomer, unfolding its white or yellow petals to attract night-flying pollinating insects, then withering before the next noon if the sun is bright; but as they wither the flowers turn color, the white ones becoming pink, the yellow ones orange or reddish.

Every turn of Zion Canyon gives a new, startling view, both ahead and behind. Cliffs and high mesas tower above the floor—some yellow, red, or pink, some topped with a white crown of sandstone. The color in the cliffs derives from the rock itself, or from vegetation, surface stains, and lichens. The dominant color is red, from the iron and manganese in the sandstone, but stretches of deep brownish-red seem to have been coated with blackish varnish; this is the famous Wingate sandstone. As the sun shifts throughout the day, the hues change, intensifying or fusing with colors reflected from peaks set aglow by the sun.

Of all the peaks forming the walls of Zion Canyon, the Great White Throne is the most singular and imposing. I look up at the monolith rising 2,400 feet above the canyon floor, following the colors as they range from deep red at the base, through pale pink and gray, to white below the forest crown on top. Zion is sometimes called the Yosemite done in oils,

in which case the Great White Throne is Half Dome in color.

From the foot of Cable Mountain I follow the trail that leads up the flank of Weeping Rock, an aptly named phenomenon that sheds its "tears" down the rock face. Where, I wonder, in this semidesert does the water originate, that sends me ducking into overhangs to avoid the shower on the trail? On inquiry I learn that snow and rain fallen on the plateau above sink slowly into the porous sandstone, then percolate downward until meeting a resistant, harder stratum through which they cannot pass; so the water can only move across the top of the layer to find its outlet, then draining in weeping fashion along the seep or spring line.

I note the striking pockets of lush green vegetation, called "hanging gardens," in moist alcoves under protective overhanging cliffs on the steep walls. Great banks of maidenhair fern occur along these crevices; clumps of pink-flowering shooting star, scarlet monkey flower, and cliff columbine flourish, along with violets and giant helleborine orchids. That seeds should be carried upward by the wind, lodge in moss or lichens on the rock surface, germinate, take root, and grow is a marvel of nature to behold; yet luxuriant hanging gardens are as much a part of southern Utah as the dry red-rock surroundings.

VIRGIN RIVER COTTONWOODS >

Beyond the splintered crimson formation called the Organ and Angels Landing rising 1,500 feet behind it, the canyon narrows and the road ends at the Temple of Sinawava, a huge natural amphitheater. From here I follow the Virgin River on foot up the narrow canyon. High cliffs, seeps, and springs offer a cool, moist environment, thriving on the sun's brief penetration. Every turn in the canyon wall gives a fresh view of hanging gardens, while cottonwood, box elder, and desert ash grow along the banks. I hear the shrill "cheep" of a canyon wren, then catch sight of this lively white-breasted bird flitting from rock to rock in search of food. Tracks of lizards and birds decorate the sandy banks.

A long trip covering 12 miles of the narrow canyon usually begins from the opposite direction and is done mostly by wading. The trip is dangerous during spring due to runoffs, and during summer due to sudden storms. Within a few hours the Virgin can become a raging torrent, uprooting and moving logs, rocks, and other debris, plainly showing that sculpturing forces are still at work.

Heading back in the soft, cool twilight, I hear the strange noises of canyon tree frogs, amplified by narrow walls to sound like a herd of sheep or goats. Darkness comes early to the canyon, and even the Great White Throne ahead is in the shadows, except for a thin strip of sunshine at its top. As quickly as the nighthawk turns in the sky, the sun leaves this huge white sandstone cliff, moving mysteriously into space, leaving the whole canyon in gathering dusk. I look behind to the hanging gardens; they too have lost their glory. Only the roar of the river remains.

In another section of the park I drive along the Kolob Canyons Road, which "opened up," as the saying goes, a magnificent area at great cost in construction, maintenance, and scars on mountain slopes. It seemed to be the thing to do, to build highways to accommodate crowds rather than reserve the special quiet and solitude of the "heavenly city of God." The Kolob section, formerly a national monument, became a part of Zion National Park in 1956; the park itself was established in 1919.

After Justice William O. Douglas had walked and waded and camped and meditated his way through the heart of Zion, he said that he had experienced a symphony, a symphony of wilderness. He felt that only those who choose to get lost in it, cutting all ties with civilization, can hear the same music.

With due credit, I don't think he's right. It isn't necessary to go to the mountain. To know that it is there in natural glory provides symphonic inspiration in itself.

GREAT WHITE THRONE

Bryce Canyon National Park

A GOVERNMENT SURVEYOR, T. C. BAILEY, STOOD AT THE RIM OF BRYCE CANYON IN 1876, A TIME when the high plateaus of southern Utah were known only to the Paiute Indians and a handful of trappers, geographers, and hardy Mormon farmers. He was overcome by what he called "the wildest and most wonderful scene that the eye of man ever beheld."

I'm not sure just where Surveyor Bailey stood, though it may well have been Inspiration Point. He noted that the surface breaks off several hundred feet almost straight down, seeming as though the bottom had dropped out and left thousands of rocks standing "in all shapes and forms as lone sentinels over grotesque and picturesque scenes."

More than a century later my view is essentially the same as Mr. Bailey's, as I identify what appear to be castles and cathedrals, monks and priests, chessmen awaiting the next move, and entire miniature cities—a fantasy of rock sculpture in colors of red, white, purple, and vermillion. In all the National Park System, I know of no landscape so delicately carved or vividly colored.

It was Major John Wesley Powell, one-armed explorer of the Grand Canyon, who initiated the scientific investigations of the valleys and plateaus of southern and central Utah in 1871. His route began at Kanab, ascended Johnson Canyon, then crossed the deeply trenched streams rising in the plateau walls of what is now the national park.

Then a group of Mormons moved down from Salt Lake City in 1874 to settle the valley east of Bryce Canyon. They were part of the movement to colonize southern Utah, which they called "Dixie Land," in hopes of developing large-scale cotton plantations. One of them, Ebenezer Bryce, pushed farther upstream from Cannonville and tried raising cattle. Though he gave it up and departed, Bryce left his name and his immortal summary of Bryce Canyon: "A hell of a place to lose a cow!"

Glowing press reports and public enthusiasm led to the establishment of Bryce Canyon National Monument in 1923, and a year later it became Utah National Park. The park was given its present name in 1928, after which its area was increased a number of times.

QUEEN'S CASTLE ALONG QUEEN'S GARDEN TRAIL

Approaching from the north, on the only road into the park, I drive leisurely along the canyon rim. Since the entire Rim Drive covers only 20 miles, I could do it in two or three hours, even allowing time to stop at the overlooks, and be on my way; but how, then, could I appreciate or comprehend the forces that have shaped this special place? I need to stay, to absorb the views from the rim and then to hike the trails below it.

Stopping at one overlook after another, I feel a cool breeze sweeping across the canyon rim. It makes me conscious of the rising elevation along the route, from 7,586 feet at Fairyland View to 8,296 feet at Bryce Point and 9,105 feet at Rainbow Point, where the road ends at the south. The summer day is pleasant, yet I learn that the first freeze of autumn will come in August, snows normally continue through May, and snowflakes may fall anytime of year. It reminds me of the great variations in terrain and climate in the mountains of southern Utah, and of how climate itself contributes to the setting and mood.

Each observation point overlooks a minor amphitheater of distinctive domes, temples, and spires. How they came to be is one of geology's marvels. Once this entire area was a large inland sea, fed by rivers and streams from surrounding highlands. Sand, silt, and lime washed into the sea and over long periods of time compacted into layers of rock. Then pressures shifted blocks of the earth's crust. The land rose from what was then sea level to mountainous heights.

Like giant platforms, some portions of southern Utah were pushed to higher elevations than others, even while other forces began to break and bend the emerging land. Then wind, snow, ice, frost, and rain exercised their influences. Cliffs started to crumble and erode into spires and pinnacles, the softer shales and sandstones giving way first, but even the more resistant limestone and siltstone ultimately yielding with undercutting of weaker layers at their base.

With every cloud shadow, the tableau of form and color looks new and different. With every summer storm, every spring snowmelt, and every day of the year, the landscape changes. Even the rim on which I stand is slowly eroding westward, giving way as an ocean beach surrenders to the force of the sea.

Chipmunks chirping shrilly and golden-mantled ground squirrels congregate in numbers near the observation points and around the picnic tables, begging for a handout. They would be better off without it, but, alas, such are the side effects of bringing civilization to the wild country. White-throated swifts and

QUEEN VICTORIA FORMATION

violet-green swallows sweep past the rim, adding to the sense of harmony, or interplay, among living and nonliving things.

Vegetation along the rim changes with rising elevation. Around North Campground and the Visitor Center ponderosa pines are abundant. With its rich, resinous aroma and its plated brownish-orange bark, the sturdy ponderosa brings a cheeriness to western mountains. In the forest near the campground I hear the chattering *pit-tick* of the western tanager and look up to see a colorful male perched on a high ponderosa limb. The ground is carpeted with thickets of manzanita, its bright green leaves and mahogany-red bark glistening under shafts of reflected sunlight. Chipmunks, squirrels, and birds all dine on its red berries.

In the higher elevations Douglas fir is the common tree, though nowhere near as towering as in the coastal regions and Cascades of the Pacific Northwest. There is white fir too, a massive tree, which I identify by the dense, heavily foliaged crown, the comparatively smooth gray bark of young trees and thick, furrowed bark of the old ones. Then there's the blue spruce, one of the most beautiful trees of the high places, with its symmetrical, pyramidal crown and crisp bluish-green foliage. Americans everywhere know it as an orna-

mental, but there's something special about seeing the tree in its natural environment.

From Rainbow Point, highest overlook on the rim, a sweeping view unfolds. The rim itself is the jagged eastern edge of the Paunsaugunt Plateau, one of the seven high "tables" of land dominating southern Utah. I can see virtually all of Bryce Canyon carved out of the formation called the Pink Cliffs, beyond to the east the 10,000-foot peaks of Table Cliff Plateau, and even faintly the Henry Mountains, 90 miles away. And southeast, across the White Cliffs and Vermilion Cliffs, the horizon reaches to the red buttes, cliffs, and mesas of Arizona. Little wonder that conservationists are trying to protect this open country as a sanctuary of clean air.

Evenings are cool in the campground. So are mornings, but one needs to rise early to properly see the yellow evening primrose, Bryce Canyon's night-blooming beauty. It will wither and fade during the heat of the day, but I am in time to observe and enjoy its lemon-yellow blossoms as broad as a teacup, speckled with droplets of morning dew. The primrose seldom grows over six inches above the ground. It's one of the fragile wild flowers that race through summer life cycles, starting with the star lily that opens in delicate white

blossoms while patches of snow still persist in the May forest.

The maze of spires holds hidden places that I realize can be seen only on the hiking trails lacing the Canyon. Considering the high elevation of the terrain and diminished available oxygen in the atmosphere, it pays to move deliberately at a slower pace than normal. And whenever I look at a trail headed down into a canyon I know the toughest part will be climbing back up.

Queen's Garden Trail, starting from Sunset Point, is the easiest trail below the rim, but it's fascinating in every way. I follow it down the switchbacks to the figure called Queen Victoria holding court with ladies-in-waiting and nobles in a garden of stone, then walk through a tunnel to Queen's Castle and Gulliver's Castle—fanciful modern names given to the spires, whereas the Paiutes described the whole array simply as "red rocks standing like men in a bowl-shaped canyon."

The ground slopes in every direction. It's a harsh environment for trees and other plants. The rapid erosion that creates the fantastic formations undermines roots and covers trees and plant stems with mud and rock, making it difficult for plant species to survive and reproduce. Nevertheless, bristlecone pines—dwarfed, misshapen, and weatherbeaten—are scattered on thin, rocky soil along the trail. While bristlecones are normally found on windswept slopes above 8,000 feet, those in Bryce Canyon are at the lowest-known elevation of their entire range.

The combined Navajo Trail and Peek-a-Boo Trail loop, also starting from Sunset Point, is more strenuous, but well worth the effort for close-up views of richly colored formations such as Thor's Hammer, the Camel and Wiseman, narrow-canyoned Wall Street, Bryce Temple, and Hindu Temples. Along the base of the towering Wall of Windows, I pause to focus attention on the colors in the rock. They derive from minerals: the reds and yellows from iron oxides and purple from manganese, while the white rocks are relatively mineral-free. Yet there is artificial coloring too. Yielding to rain or snowmelt, sediment runs down from overlying layers of red rock to coat white lime and siltstone layers below. The red silt in the dripping clings to the new surface like a thin coat of natural stucco, creating an effect on the Bryce Canyon walls of cave stalactites and hot springs formations.

The scene constantly changes. Old formations crumble, as did Oastler Castle, a favorite arch on the Fairyland Loop that collapsed under its own weight in the 1960s, and new ones emerge in this marvelous wild fantasia.

Arches National Park

THE WIND SWEEPS ACROSS MY FACE AND OVER THE MESA TOP. THERE IS ALMOST ALWAYS A blowing wind, a constant reminder of the harsh character of the land in southeastern Utah. At the edge of precipitous red cliffs, Delicate Arch vaults above the mesa to a height greater than that of a seven-story building. I scrutinize this fantasy in stone and marvel at its form, composition, and history. Geologists have calculated that it took at least 70,000 years for the wind, combined with the forces of frost, rain, and sun, to sculpt this tapered freestanding arch.

I climb very slowly down the steep trail over slickrock scarred with potholes that are filled with rain from thundershowers of the night before. All around me in the red-rock country of Arches National Park are the buttes, mesas, canyons, and steep-walled cliffs that typify the untamed Southwest, or what's left of it. Then I continue to walk amid a galaxy of natural arches, windows, spires, balanced rocks, and figures resembling men and animals carved in rock; more of these formations are located in Arches National Park than anywhere else in America. Though its scenic grandeur was formerly protected as a national monument, the national park was established only in 1971.

I hike up dry "washes" of desert streams and over reddish sand dunes. At one bend in a canyon I find an entire bank decorated with the western cardinal flower, or lobelia, its deep red blossoms framed against a sandstone cliff.

Soil, grasses, and trees may be scant, but I am continually reminded of the vitality and life implicit in the desert. Showy blossoms of penstemon, phlox, paintbrush, sand lupine, yucca, cactus, daisies, and mariposa lilies bring color to spring and early summer, except in very dry years. The signs of wildlife are everywhere in Arches. Overhead a golden eagle soars and wheels, while sharing the skies with red-tailed hawks, ravens, doves, and horned larks. Beavers leave their tracks in sandy streambeds. Deer, coyotes, and foxes, most active at night, leave their tracks too. One of the most unusual animals, the kangaroo rat, gets its name from outsize hind legs that help it to escape from enemies by leaping like a tiny kangaroo. This little rodent wags a tail longer than the rest of its body, and it is so fitted for the desert that it can go through its entire life without taking a drink of water, which is more than any of us humans can do.

Deep in the park I follow a trail to a series of beautifully sculptured arches. Some of these, the Double-O for instance, are aptly named. Like abstract paintings, others might be given any names that come to mind, but along this route they are called Pine Tree, Partition, Skyline, Dark Angel, and Landscape. Spanning 291 feet, Landscape is the longest natural stone arch known to exist, but what strikes me most is that at one point it's only six feet thick. The arch should hardly be able to support its own weight, yet there it stands.

In the section called The Windows I observe eight immense arches as well as many smaller ones. Among the famous formations here are the Double Arch, the Balanced Rock, and the Parade of Elephants. Some 90 arches of varying size have been discovered; doubtless there are others in less easily penetrated areas of the park. At the lower end of Devils Garden, in the part of the park known as the Fiery Furnace, I behold a great jumble of vertical slabs of red rock that glows in the light cast by the setting sun.

The rock itself was deposited as sand about 150 million years ago, during the Jurassic period. Ancient upheavals warped the earth's crust upward to form an anticline, an arch of stratified rock some 30 miles in length. Then the crest of the huge fold sank, forming what are now known as Salt Valley and Cache Valley. Water entering cracks in the rock dissolved some of the cementing material. Then water and wind removed the loose sand, forming thin fins of soft sandstone. More rapid wearing of softer areas in vertical walls resulted in undercutting, while carving by water and frost has continued to this day. In due course, this thinning by weather will bring the collapse of the graceful, smoothly contoured arches. For the present I can observe all stages in the process of development and decay.

Arches contains the remains of roads built for mining and grazing before the national park was established. One of these roads leads to the pioneer Turnbow Cabin on Salt Creek near Delicate Arch. But in this raw country of harsh climate and rugged terrain human population has always been sparse. "I cannot conceive of a more worthless and impracticable region than the one we now find ourselves in," reported Captain John N. Macomb, who led a party into the area in 1859.

In the years that followed, cattle ranching emerged, despite scantiness of forage. The industry gave rise to outlaw bands, such as Butch Cassidy and his Wild Bunch, and to cattle empires. In recent times ranching and farming have been replaced by mining for uranium, potash, oil, and natural gas, and by tourism—all centered around Moab, the old Mormon town, five miles south of the entrance to Arches National Park.

The towering sandstone formations and deep chasms that remained impassable for so long have now lost their defenses. There are

TURNBOW CABIN ON SALT CREEK

LANDSCAPE ARCH

scenic flights, jeep tours, river trips, and roads into the backcountry of southern Utah. Glen Canyon, once one of the wildest areas, is now the setting of Lake Powell, a man-made reservoir named, ironically, for Major John Wesley Powell, who led a daring expedition down the Colorado River more than a century ago. Before the reservoir was completed in 1963, the trip to Rainbow Bridge National Monument—encompassing the largest, most perfect natural bridge in the world, with an implicit archi-

tectural beauty—demanded an expedition in itself. Now Rainbow Bridge can be reached by boat and a one-mile walk.

As I move among canyons, cliffs, and pinnacles, I realize that the same ruggedness that gives this country its beauty has also given it protection from the advance of man. Now it is for the national parks to sustain the safeguards, and I am pleased that some of Arches' treasures are still tucked away in unroaded, unexplored portions.

Overhead the clouds darken, heavy with thundershowers soon to fall. Shadows creep up the canyon walls. Weather and climate are part of the land and give a feeling to it, whether it be the minus-20-degree winter temperature, the spring sandstorms, or the sudden summer outbursts. The flash floods will follow, rearranging the landscape, and after them another show of flowers to lend contrast to the red rocks and the snowy peaks high above them.

TURRET ARCH THROUGH NORTH WINDOW (TOP)
AND DOUBLE ARCH, ARCHES NATIONAL PARK

Capitol Reef National Park

OF ALL THE NATIONAL PARKS, CAPITOL REEF IS PROBABLY THE LEAST KNOWN, WHICH gives it a rather pleasant distinction. Yellowstone and Yosemite and other national parks have grown so prominent in the public eye and so accessible that few secrets about them still remain. It's good to have at least one place in America with a little mystery left to it, a puzzler.

South-central Utah is a strange, little-known land. Development is scant. Due east, Moab, the gateway to Arches and Canyonlands national parks, has grown into a tourist hub. So has Cedar City to the west, which provides access to Zion and Bryce Canyon national parks and Cedar Breaks National Monument. There are no such focal points around Capitol Reef. The entire region is changing, with development of energy resources, to electrify distant cities, but Capitol Reef and its environs have seen the least change—that is, until now.

Tilted cliffs and rainbow-hued rocks rise above the desert, not solely in the national park but also in the public domain and national forest that surround it. A national park represents purely a formal designation by a group of men, based on subjective value judgments or political considerations. The earth itself knows no such classification. Thus I feel little restraint in admiring features outside the park as well as those within.

Only one road crosses this slender north-south-lying park. Following the road as it cuts across the northern portion, I stop at the Goosenecks lookout, facing the deep zigzag canyon carved by the Fremont River, and begin to observe the outline and components of the "reef," a 20-mile-long earth uplift that rises 1,000 feet and more above the river. Early geologists apparently called such cliffs "reefs" because of their resemblance to coral formations. But over the years water and wind have carved a fantastic array of domes, towers, and pinnacles in the rock of Capitol Reef. It's the white-capped domelike peaks in the Navajo sandstone that account for the "Capitol" in the park's name.

Following nearby trails, I hike up the Grand Wash between canyon walls displaying rock formations, as well as pictographs left by the Anasazi, the "Ancient Ones," forefathers of the Indians we know now. I continue up a steep course to the high cliffs and Cassidy Arch, named for Butch Cassidy, the outlaw, who used this country as a hiding place. Such traces of adventurous history tell the story of man against a tough, unyielding land. South of Grand Wash, passing thousands of potholes, I reach Capitol Gorge, where Indian petroglyphs share the rock with the carved names of pioneers who utilized the enormous natural water tanks. What, I wonder, were their dreams, their regrets, their thoughts on finding natural spectacles in this expansive, unexploited country?

Cathedral Valley, north of the highway, demands a vehicle with four-wheel drive. My friends and I cross the dusty plains through the Valley of Decision, a narrow gap so named because a driver must choose whether to proceed or, in the face of clouds and threatening skies, turn back. The arid climate makes the park susceptible to long droughts, which dry up seeps, springs, and water pockets. Then a sudden shower may send tons of water hurtling down a narrow canyon. Once inside the

SANDSTONE "CASTLE"

Valley of Decision, a person is trapped during a flash flood; even with a moderate rain, if the driver gets across he may still be stranded at least a few hours.

Fortunately, the skies are fleeced with high stratus clouds on a relatively cool day that will see no showers. In Cathedral Valley our effort is rewarded by the spectacle of huge monoliths of reddish-brown sandstone capped with grayish-yellow strata, bearing such names as Temple of the Sun, Queen of the Wash, Giant's Armchair, Walls of Jericho, and Gunsight Dike. Beyond these colorful "cathedrals," many of them freestanding on the valley floor, rise the Fish Lake Mountains,

with Thousand Lake Mountain, more than 11,300 feet, towering above all. Within so short a span the landscape can change from deep, dry canyons to sparsely vegetated plateaus to high forests and windy reaches.

The Reef is a scenic spur of the Waterpocket Fold, a strip of tilted and exposed rock layers almost 70 miles long, extending from Thousand Lake Mountain, just outside the park, southeast to the Colorado River at Glen Canyon. This huge ridge derives the second part of its name from a great folding of the earth's crust, in a classic monocline; the first part signifies the shallow depressions which collect

rainwater and hold it for long periods as a boon to man and animal alike. I cross the Fold south of the highway, over the Burr Trail, an old cattle-drive route still unpaved, with switchbacks and steep grades. Along the way I encounter fascinating sandstone forms and canyons and the spectacular outcrops of the Sleeping Rainbow formation—stretching for miles like a lazy, sprawling rainbow along the face of the Circle Cliffs.

Capitol Reef itself was a national monument for many years. The area, enlarged to embrace all of the Waterpocket Fold, was designated a national park in 1971 and given the protection it well deserves.

UPPER CATHEDRAL VALLEY

Canyonlands National Park

THE COLORADO RIVER AND ITS MAJOR TRIBUTARY, THE GREEN, MERGE IN THE HEART OF CANyonlands National Park. Together they have been the most powerful force in shaping Canyonlands' flaming mass of red-rock canyons and sandstone walls. For ages upon ages these streams have been slicing through rock, stripping back the layers, and carrying away endless tons of sand and silt in a process as natural as the procreation of living species.

Seen from Grandview Point atop the mesa called Island in the Sky, in the north district of the park, the two rivers, a thousand feet below, seem to be almost buried in the twisting gorges and embedding themselves deeper still. I look across the land between the rivers, an array of bold soaring buttes, the immediate part of a panorama of hundreds of square miles of rocky wilderness reaching to the blue mountains at the horizon.

For generations Canyonlands was little known and barely explored, even though Zane Grey had set many of his novels in the nearby Mormon town of Moab. The establishment of the national park in 1964 set aside a portion of the canyon country that contains some of the most striking examples of geological erosion on earth.

Marvels are abundant in southeast Utah, each one different and worthy of preservation in its own right. A few are protected. Dead Horse Point, just north of the national park, is a small state park overlooking all three levels of the Canyonlands—the rim of the Island in the Sky, the intermediate plateau, and the Colorado River. Huge sandstone bridges and magnificent canyons are protected in Natural Bridges National Monument, south of Canyonlands. Farther south, the serpentine gorge called the Great Goosenecks of the San Juan River is in a state reserve, close to the huge monoliths and pinnacles of aptly named Monument Valley on the Navajo Indian Reservation.

The national park was carved out of the public domain. Though belonging to the entire nation, the land had been used primarily for private livestock grazing and mineral exploration. Other superb little-known areas are still unprotected on the public domain in southern Utah. Having roved this country, I can't think of any area more worth saving than the environs of the Escalante River, a treasure of deep, narrow canyons, river-cut cliffs, natural bridges, and waterfalls leaping over sandstone ledges. Preservation of Canyonlands is a good thing, but the wild Escalante River must not be lost either.

MOLAR ROCK AND ANGEL ARCH

Possibly the most unusual feature in Canyonlands is the formation called Upheaval Dome, which lies on the Island of the Sky. A mysterious fragment of geologic history that measures three miles across and almost 1,600 feet deep in the central part, it suggests the crater of a huge multicolored volcano, or a natural amphitheater. Theories that Upheaval was caused by a meteor or possibly by an underground gas explosion are no longer seriously considered; the generally accepted explanation today defines it as a salt dome, similar to the ones found in the Louisiana-Texas oil fields and in Iran, but more exposed.

As I follow the trail around the inner crater rim, I realize that whatever its origin Upheaval Dome is plainly something different even in a world of different things, like an abstraction in a gallery of forms and figures. Its colors have their own explanation, if I dare to reduce abstraction to science. Major formations of rock, dating to the ancient salt sea and the "Age of Reptiles," once lay in horizontal layers; now they have been tilted on edge by the flow of salt and revealed like the rings of a cut onion. Navajo sandstone, the bold red of Whale Rock atop the canyon, is the youngest formation, deposited as a 2,000-foot-thick layer of windblown sand. Banded purple, green, and gray Moenkopi around the base of the crater, circling the 500-foot spires pushed up from the White Rim layer below, is the oldest.

The walls of Canyonlands are decorated with rock pictographs and petroglyphs left by the Anasazi a thousand years ago. On the gravel road to the Needles section of the na-

tional park, I stop at Newspaper Rock, a state historical monument, to ponder the carvings on the face of the rock. The men and animals, houses and hunters, circles, snakes, and symbolic rivers must have meant something to the Indians who scratched them on the wall. Directional markers, perhaps? An identification of property? And how will some future time interpret our culture from what we leave behind?

Reminders of the Anasazi are everywhere. In parts of Canyonlands storehouses of grain, with the corn in them dried iron-hard by a thousand summers, are still standing as they were left. Palm prints are visible on the walls of caves. In Salt Creek Canyon, the intriguing rock painting dubbed the "All-American Man" looks down with a smile and a challenge to science and the imagination.

There is a lesson to be learned even now from the partnership between the Anasazi and their land, though drought finally forced them to leave. They met the desert on its own terms —not on theirs. Thus they were able to live in the Southwest for more than ten centuries, more than three of them in the Canyonlands area, pursuing pottery, weaving, and basketry, hunting bighorn sheep, deer, and small game, without altering the balance of nature in their surroundings.

I travel by jeep, then hike in the Needles section, where massive sandstone has been worn into clusters of pillars, spires, arches, balanced rocks, and steeples. From Elephant Hill I observe soaring rocks that stand against the sky like 30-story skyscrapers. The landscape is

splashed and banded by brilliant rainbow hues. Angel Arch, near the "All-American Man" in Salt Creek Canyon, has an opening 190 feet high. I try to compare it with the colossal Arc de Triomphe in Paris, which measures 164 feet to its summit. Druid Arch, squarer than the others, suggests three balanced Druid stones that might have been taken from Stonehenge on the Salisbury Plain, but instead of being twice as high as a man can reach, these are about 250 feet tall.

In some places clusters of jumbled needles render areas a mile or more across virtually impenetrable. Chesler Park, a grassy arena, is totally encircled by pinnacles suggesting sandstone deities. In the Grabens—fault valleys caused by subsurface dissolution or movement of salt—the land looks like it might have been dropped down an elevator shaft, leaving behind flat-stoned surfaces bordered by vertical walls. Surrounding distances are so immense that the deep faults in the earth's crust deceptively appear smaller than they are.

Looking closer, I notice smooth caves hollowed out of the softer rock layers, resembling giant swallows' nests. Many broad rock faces are patterned with lichens, colored variously dark, light, or blue-gray, tinged with pink, some shaped like crescents, others like doughnuts—tiny points of tenacious, determined plant life. Then there's "desert varnish," colored from yellow to deep brown, caused by water seeping for century after century from rock walls in weeping fashion. The sandstone cross-bedding makes it seem as though nature has sculptured an endless variety of friezes and bas-reliefs.

There is little water in this country. Springs are infrequent, soils are thin, vegetation sparse. Because of underlying salt beds, most groundwater is brine. Still, hardy junipers and pinyon pine grow in the bottomlands and between big sandstone boulders. Water trickling off rock faces provides the trees a little extra.

High above their junction, I see the Colorado and Green rivers running brown with silt. Oddly, I recall being some years earlier in the mountains of western Wyoming where plunging streams merge to form the headwaters of the Green and finding that the color really is green, due to milky glacial particles suspended in the water. Now the Green will flow wildly with the Colorado through Cataract Canyon before being slowed down and pacified by Glen Canyon Dam. Canyonlands, happily, is free of such development. Or, as an early explorer reported of Cataract, here grandeur, glory, and desolation are all merged into one.

< OVERLEAF: STANDING ROCKS BASIN FROM GRANDVIEW POINT

Petrified Forest National Park

NORTH OF THE LITTLE COLORADO RIVER IN EAST-CENTRAL ARIZONA, I DRIVE ACROSS THE Painted Desert, a wide, arid land of plateaus, buttes, and low mesas lavishly displaying vibrant colors in bands of sandstones, shales, and clays. The vivid hues seem appropriate to the Indian heartland of Navajo, Hopi, Apache, and Zuni.

It is almost impossible to conceive that in place of these high, arid plateaus with scanty plant growth and receiving less than ten inches of moisture yearly, a forest once grew in a low-lying basin; that beds of ferns, mosses, and cycads looking somewhat like modern palms thrived in marshlands and along streams, while conifers flourished in scattered groves on hills and ridges above the water.

So it was in the Triassic period, about 200 million years ago, before upheavals and mountain-making sequences lifted the land several thousand feet. I find vestiges of the ancient landscape at Petrified Forest, where there's really no forest at all, but rather the largest and most colorful concentration of petrified wood in the world, a galaxy of stone trees so hard that they can scratch all but the hardest alloy steels.

The most colorful portion of the Painted Desert comprises the north section of Petrified Forest National Park. In the south section of the park are the best "forests."

The national park consists of six separate "forests," each with great chips, chunks, and logs of onyx, agate, and jasper strewn across the ground. One of them, Black Forest, a concentrated deposit of dark petrified wood, is in the Painted Desert section. In Rainbow Forest, near the south entrance of the park, the piles of long logs, many exceeding 100 feet in length, are most revealing of the petrification process. It is believed that the trees were transported by flooding streams from surrounding highlands to be buried under mud and sand, then covered by layers of silica-rich volcanic ash. The silica and other minerals gradually filled in the wood cells until the logs virtually turned to stone. Traces of iron, manganese, and carbon stained the silica to form the present colors. After the forest was buried and upheavals had lifted the land, wind and rain removed the sediment covers to expose a portion of the logs. Countless other logs are believed to be buried below the surface, to a depth of 300 feet.

At the beautiful Blue Mesa, colorful banded buttes, cones, and mesas clearly reveal ancient layers of marsh. Erosion nibbling at the soft earth here and elsewhere in the park has left some petrified logs stranded in unusual positions on slender pedestals. Ultimately they tumble from their perches to stimulate erosion anew. Eagles' Nest Rock, one of the most famous landmarks in the park, collapsed in the 1930s. Indians tell that for as long as their ancestors could remember, eagles used the top of the rock for nesting. They did not return at the usual time preceding the fall of the formation, obeying perhaps some built-in premonition.

Near Jasper Forest, so called for the opaque colors of some of the "wood," is Agate Bridge, a single mammoth log straddling a deep ravine. In aptly named Long Logs forest, the petrified logs may be 160 feet long. Close by, overlooking Rainbow Forest, is the Agate House, a partially restored Indian pueblo that was built of colorful petrified wood chunks many centuries ago.

Petrified Forest was barely known until the railroads opened the age of settlement late in the nineteenth century. Once discovered, this out-of-the-way corner was mobbed by souvenir hunters, gem collectors, and commercial jewelers. Digging, dynamiting, hauling away petrified wood in huge quantities, they showed the earth no mercy. Crystal Forest was a special target, many of its logs destroyed for the gem-quality quartz crystals they contain. Fortunately there were no bulldozers then. And when a mill was built to crush logs into abrasives, public outrage led to federal protection of the area—first as a national monument and later, in 1962, as a national park.

PEDESTAL LOG

Though it could be worse, the vandalism has never ended. The park is filled with signs warning and pleading against removing pieces of loose petrified wood, yet people continue doing it. But why? What is the root of this acquisitive, destructive urge?

In late afternoon I watch colors change across the Painted Desert, as though in motion —earth, sky, and clouds together gathering me up to flow through space with them. I can take everything I need and want from here without removing a thing.

PETRIFIED FRAGMENTS IN RAINBOW FOREST

PEDESTAL LOG IN THE BLUE MESA

Carlsbad Caverns National Park

NO TWO CAVES ARE EVER THE SAME. THEY MAY HAVE SIMILAR FORMATIONS, YET EACH is distinct, reflecting its own natural environment over long periods of time. Caves are still being discovered, though they have existed for eons, and large portions of known caves have never been fully explored.

In the case of Carlsbad, the big brother of all the rest, its caverns have been explored to a depth of more than 1,000 feet, but this is only the beginning. More than 60 caves of varying dimensions lie within the national park, which is located in southeastern New Mexico, but development has been limited to the mighty Carlsbad Cavern. Other portions are reserved for research; some have never been fully explored.

I appreciate the world underground and try to absorb its meaning as well as the unusual spectacles it displays. Walking through Carlsbad, I am amazed to observe, imbedded in the crystalline limestone, red chert and fossil remains of varied invertebrate life forms more than 200 million years old. Their existence is no accident, since the limestone was once part of the Capitan Reef edging a salt-water basin that covered part of Texas and New Mexico. In time the reef was buried under layers of sediment, then raised to form the foothills of the Guadalupe Mountains, under which huge caves were formed by rainwater seeping through cracks and dissolving away the rock.

In the Big Room I stand in the largest underground gallery in the world, with a ceiling as high as a 25-story building and floor space for 14 football fields. There is much to see and contemplate in this chamber alone, yet my thoughts wander to caves elsewhere in America. Three caves—Carlsbad, Mammoth, and Wind—are national parks, and three others—Timpanogos, Oregon, and Jewel—national monuments. Jewel was an obscure preserve in South Dakota until recent years, when it was discovered to be the fourth-longest cave in the world, with formations of breathtaking beauty. The Forest Service unearthed Blanchard Caverns under the surface of Ozark National Forest in Arkansas; that agency developed the cave quite carefully with protection of the ecosystem in mind, while heedlessly stripping trees from the ground above and pouring in doses of chemical poisons. Missouri's Ozarks contain the greatest collection of caves in the world. I recall visiting Meramec Caverns, where Jesse James presumably hid out, and finding a carnival arrangement drawing huge throngs. Onondaga, on the other hand, one of the largest and loveliest of

them all, has been preserved essentially in its natural condition. Curiously, both were owned by the same man. In Virginia, Shenandoah Valley is cave country too. Luray, largest of the Virginia caverns, though a commercial operation, is done well, for it preserves the resource and introduces many people to nature underground.

As for the Big Room of Carlsbad, its formations are of endless variety and beauty and color. Some stalactites hang from the ceiling like fragile chandeliers or waterfalls frozen in stone. One formation, poised over the path, is called, appropriately, the Sword of Damocles. Stalagmites rise from the floor in myriad shapes, the formations bearing such names as Totem Poles, Twin Domes, and Temple of the Sun. Here too, in a dark central alcove, is the celebrated Rock of Ages. Among the most beautiful of the smaller chambers are the Green Lake Room, named for a small green pool, the King's Palace, the Queen's Chamber, and the Papoose Room.

During the 1880s ranchers and settlers referred to the part of the cave then visible as Bat Cave. They were content to let the bats have it as their special place until easily mined, nitrate-rich bat guano attracted attention, and thousands of tons were extracted for agricultural fertilizer. One of the miners, Jim White, a local boy, went exploring beyond the bat caves armed only with a kerosene lamp and discovered the marvels underground. Presently visitors thronged this remote attraction, though in the early days it meant entering via miner's bucket lowered several hundred feet to the cavern floor. Set aside as a national monument in 1923, Carlsbad was designated a national park in 1930.

Tourists have fared better than bats. Once these great divers and flyers numbered in the millions. They would spend the day hanging head downward in dense clusters from the walls and ceiling, then spiral outward for night-long feeding on insects in the surrounding valleys. Alas, the great bat population has

TEMPLE OF THE SUN IN THE BIG ROOM

82

ENTRANCE TO KING'S PALACE

sharply declined for reasons not fully under-
stood, though likely including extermination
of their roosting caves in Mexico, warming
and drying of the cave (caused by using cave
air to air-condition the Visitor Center), and,
above all, the widespread application of pesti-
cides. Bats do a better job of eliminating crop-
destroying insects and are cleaner than pesti-
cides. One day we may learn.

Guadalupe Mountains National Park

IN 1925, J. C. HUNTER, A JUDGE OF CULBERSON COUNTY, TEXAS, PICKED UP ONE SECTION OF LAND in the wide, open spaces west of the Pecos River. His parcel was closer to Carlsbad, New Mexico, about 55 miles northeast, than to any town in Texas. In due course he and his son acquired large additional holdings on the slopes of the Guadalupes, a range that rises boldly, like an island, above the Chihuahuan desert. The Hunters put the land to use, raising Angora goats to produce mohair wool, but were careful to avoid overgrazing, in anticipation that one day the land would become part of a national park.

Forty years later, in 1965, I am at the Hunter ranch, which is still being grazed by goats. The national park is not yet established, though plainly in sight at last. "I hold title to the land, but how can anyone consider himself owner of this magnificent country when these mountains have stood alone here for millions of years?" asks J. C. Hunter, Jr., rhetorically, expressing in a soft but firm voice a view that goes to the root of man's relationship to the earth. It contrasts sharply with the prevailing Texas philosophy that God-given resources are meant to be used, not saved.

Hunter, during the course of conversation at the ranch house, cites the role of Wallace E. Pratt, who began purchasing property among the cliffs and canyons of the Guadalupes before Judge Hunter did. As a practicing geologist, Pratt appreciated the distinction of the Guadalupe Mountains as part of the Capitan Reef, dating from the ancient Permian period, when a vast saltwater basin occupied a large portion of what is now Texas and New Mexico. In fact, the 500 fossil species identified in the gray, tan, black, and olive walls of McKittrick

Canyon—where Pratt had his ranch—made the Canyon a mecca for geologists in tracing earth history, especially the origin of such valuable mineral resources as petroleum, potash, dolomite, and limestone.

Over the years Wallace Pratt became wealthy and internationally renowned as a petroleum geologist, but his interest lay in safeguarding the rich natural values in McKittrick Canyon. "We are part of the ecology, too," he wrote. "We have just as much right to live as the seals and the whales—but no more." In 1961 the federal government accepted his donation of 5,632 acres. Then J. C. Hunter moved to offer 72,000 acres, the entire "Hunter Lands," at a price of $1½ million.

Rare plant communities grow on the floor of McKittrick Canyon. One species of moss here is also found in a small region of eastern Asia but nowhere else on earth. The treelike Faxon yucca grows to heights of almost 20 feet and sometimes much higher. The Texas madrona is clothed in a satin-smooth trunk colored varying hues of gray, purple, saffron, orange, and vermillion, depending on the season of year. Unlike most trees, the madrona sheds its bark, not its leaves.

The Canyon is only one part of the park. For the ride to the summit I am offered the choice of a horse or a mule. I have been on horses many times but never on a mule. Generally on mountain trips mules are assigned to carry gear, not people, as though lacking in breeding or dignity; or perhaps they're too stubborn to fool with. I choose the mule named "Ace," brawny but not broad, and not unfriendly. Though expecting a rough gait, I find that Ace rides as smoothly and gently as a rocking chair.

From the foot of the mountains, landscaped with agaves, cacti, and yucca in many different species, I ride upward through stands of scrub oak, bigtooth maple, and alligator juniper, so easily identified by the thick, scaly bark patterned like the hide of an alligator. A coyote scoots along the trail out front, then heads cross-country over the rocks. Coyotes are despised in Texas, especially by purveyors of poison against them. In the Guadalupe Mountains, however, coyotes, bobcats, and mountain lions—the "varmints"—are protected along with more "respectable" animals, including Texas' only herd of wild elk.

Approaching the summit, I see ponderosa pine, limber pine, Douglas fir, and a few aspen spread over the most nearly level and densely forested portion of the park, a rare treat above the desert. Once on top, in an almost alpine environment, surefooted Ace leads me over the whitish-colored cliffs of 8,078-foot-high El Capitan, rising a thousand feet above the slopes at its base, but I still look up to Guadalupe Peak, over 8,700 feet in height, the highest point in Texas. I never imagined anything like it in this part of America.

In 1966 Congress, spurred by Senator Ralph Yarborough of Texas, authorized the establishment of Guadalupe Mountains National Park and the acquisition of the Hunter lands, at $21 per acre—the sort of bargain that is now rare. Senator Yarborough was a rare species himself, like the Hunters and Wallace Pratt. Most politicians like to bring their states shipyards and reservoirs; Ralph Yarborough worked to bring Texas this national park (formally established in 1972) and Padre Island National Seashore and Big Thicket National Preserve as well.

EVENING SKY OVER GUADALUPE MOUNTAINS

Big Bend
National Park

FOLLOWING THE TRAIL INTO THE CHISOS MOUNTAINS OF SOUTH-WESTERN TEXAS, THE SUREFOOTED black mare and I climb above the desert and brush. We ascend into the crags and canyons through an environment of pinyon, scrub oak, and juniper. Such vegetation I would expect here, but presently we enter an island forest of aspen, ponderosa pine, and Douglas fir, more like the North Woods than the Chihuahuan desert.

The mountains are a surprise in themselves. Upthrust 6,000 feet above the arid plains, with the highest peak 7,835 feet above sea level, the Chisos are the southernmost mountain mass in the United States. Distant from cities, even from towns, Big Bend National Park is like a last frontier, a part of the land rather than of the nation. It gives me the feeling of the old Spanish-Mexican Southwest that reaches back more than four centuries on both sides of the Rio Grande.

There are other riders with me, and when we stop to rest and reconnoiter, the naturalist in our group prowls among the rocks and thickets on a sloping hillside. Whispering, he beckons us to follow him. Presently he points to a pair of birds, sparrow-size, sequestered in the trees but fairly close to the ground. They are Colima warblers, rare birds which divide their seasons between south-central Mexico and the Chisos, hardly knowing the difference between one side of the border and the other. The Colima resembles the widespread Virginia warbler, with a few differences in color; it has a lovely lyric trill. We listen intently while the naturalist locates the reason for the warblers' presence—a nest of leaves, grass, and hair partially hidden among the rocks, with four little speckled eggs that will, I hope, forgive the intrusion.

More than 200 species of birds have been identified in the park at one time or another during the year. The park provides such diverse habitats that it can accommodate them all. The birds range from the curious cuckoo-like roadrunner, a weak flyer but swift runner, the elegant Scott's oriole among the yuccas and agaves, and the cactus wren to the heron, teal, cliff swallow, golden eagle, and, of course, the Colima warbler. Doubtless there were more species before federal protection of the area ended the heavy livestock grazing that also took its toll of the vegetation. "Every plant either sticks, stings, or stinks," the saying went, and by 1944, when the park was established, there wasn't much vegetation left on the plains and slopes. Since the departure of the large livestock herds, the plants, in a thousand different species, have come back,

and with them the life-systems they support.

On the ridgecrest known somehow as the South Rim (there is no North Rim), I encounter fields of endless space, endless time. From the bald head of the Chisos, horizons seem to go on forever with scarcely a trace of human civilization, touching the silvery Rio Grande far below, extending across the castles and cathedrals carved in rock, the tawny desert, and the rugged purple-hued Sierra del Carmen on the Mexican side, embracing the utter immensity of sky and land.

The composition of mountain, river, and desert spread before me has been shaped over millions of years. A shallow inland sea once covered the Big Bend country. When the sea receded, it left sediments of mud, sand, and lime that hardened into rock, embedding traces of shells and fossils. During a later period dinosaurs and 50-foot-long crocodiles roamed through dark marshes and tropical forests, while huge flying reptiles called pterodactyls soared overhead. Climates changed, and with them life forms. Then came a sequence of volcanic activity and mountain building, followed by erosion that shaped the rounded rocks, vertical cliffs, and deep canyons.

The Rio Grande has played its part in the sculpturing process. The river winds more than 100 miles along the southern boundary of the park—which is also the boundary between the United States and Mexico—on its great U-shaped bend, called the *gran comba* by the Mexicans. Three times on its course the river cuts through massive, dramatic canyons— Santa Elena, Mariscal, and Boquillas.

Santa Elena Canyon is a dark, winding slit that opens into a boxlike gorge with sheer 1,500-foot limestone cliffs. Here I walk along a rocky ledge into the heart of the canyon, ob-

serving the green ribbon of cottonwood, willow, and mesquite trees, reeds, shore grasses, and salt cedar that contrasts with the desert. The floodplain is frequented by many birds, including green and great blue herons, sandpipers, canyon wrens, and green-winged teals. At Castolon the river is so narrow that I could cross by ferry (a rowboat) to the little Mexican village of Santa Elena.

The adobe houses and store at Castolon reflect the region's long frontier history. Comanches rode through the Big Bend to raid isolated Spanish settlements on the Rio Grande. Following annexation of Texas by the United States, a military troop arrived in 1856 with more than 30 camels, dispatched by Secretary of War Jefferson Davis as a revolutionary mode of transport across the desert. Altogether, some 80 camels were imported, but the whole idea was scrapped with the advent of the Civil War, and the last of the animals were turned loose and vanished. The cavalry was in and out of the area after the war to protect cattlemen from Indian raids. The last wild flurry occurred in 1916, when Mexican revolutionaries invaded the United States via the Big Bend.

Except for sporadic rustling, the border has been quiet and peaceful ever since, or at least nonviolent, yet narcotics smugglers crossing the border through the park play hide-and-seek with the law, and so do Mexican laborers, the "wetbacks." While poking around one day in Boquillas Canyon, the longest and perhaps most spectacular of Big Bend's famous gorges, my friend Elmer and I happen on a candelilla camp—a delightful discovery of Rio Grande lore that frightens us both a little, considering that candelilla workers are alleged to be tough hombres resentful of company, like moon-

shiners in the Appalachians. The candelilla is a tall-growing wax plant which these men boil down in huge vats along the river in order to sell the residue for use in making polishes, paper coatings, pharmaceuticals, and cosmetics. Somehow it all becomes suspect since they apparently cut plants on the American side and process them on the Mexican. These simple men prove not the least bit hostile to Elmer and me. Their labor is elemental and hard, tougher than moonshining.

I walk through the desert at twilight, a "witching hour" when mule deer leave the arroyos to feed on open hillsides and coyotes begin their nocturnal serenade, when nighthawks swoop in to feed on rodents and great horned owls alight on long-stemmed ocotillo to await nightfall. Even without people the land is filled with life—the life of insects, lizards, snakes, turtles, tarantulas, mountain lions, and javelina. It is also filled with the life of plants, including species of the arid land better known to Mexicans than to most Americans. Among these are the lechuguilla, an agave, little sister of the century plant, from whose fibers Mexicans weave ropes, harnesses, saddlebags, and other useful things; the drooping juniper, which grows from Central America to the extreme northern limits of its range at Big Bend; the sotol, with a cluster of ribbonlike leaves and unbranched flower stalk; and the Spanish dagger, or yucca, which presents a singular spectacle of bell-like creamy blossoms in March and April.

Big Bend's images and color tones change by season and hour of day. Lava-capped Casa Grande and Tule Mountain, standing guard over Chisos Mountains Basin, absorb the purple twilight setting over the wilderness.

< OVERLEAF: ALLIGATOR JUNIPER ON
SOUTH RIM OF CHISOS MOUNTAINS

DESERT PLANTS IN CHISOS MOUNTAINS >

THE ROCKIES & THE PLAINS

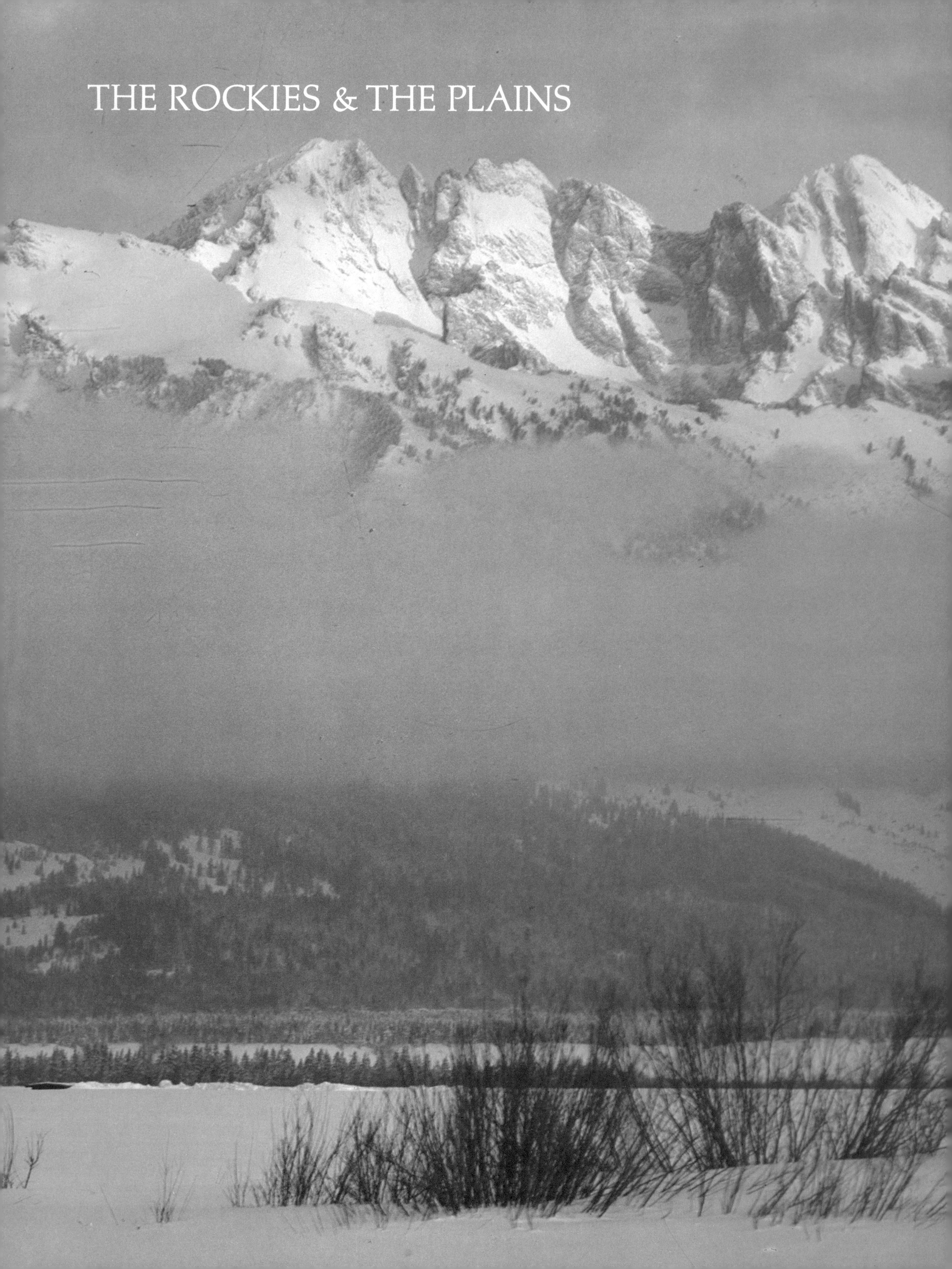

Mesa Verde National Park

ON THE MESA VERDE, THE FOR-ESTED TABLELAND AT THE EDGE OF THE SAN JUAN RANGE of the Rockies, I have come to explore silent cities built long ago, but it's impossible to view man's work as something apart from the natural environment.

The Mesa Verde—"Green Table" in Span-ish—rises abruptly above the surrounding terrain of southwestern Colorado. It com-mands the horizon for 100 miles over the Four Corners country, where the borders of Colo-rado, New Mexico, Arizona, and Utah meet. Covered with pinyon and ponderosa pines, junipers and oaks, the mesa is something of a meeting place itself, blending the feeling of mountain and desert. The south side of the tableland is honeycombed with deep canyons. It is here, in the caves and crannies of the can-yons and on the mesa tops, that hundreds of Indian villages of ages past are located. The complex is considered the most notable and best preserved pre-Columbian ruins in the United States. In fact, among all the national parks, Mesa Verde is the only one established to preserve archaeological treasures.

Prehistoric Indian ruins are widespread in Colorado, New Mexico, Arizona, and Utah. Aztec Ruins, Bandelier, Canyon de Chelly, Casa Grande, Chaco Canyon, Gila Cliff Dwellings, Gran Quivira, Hovenweep, Monte-zuma Castle, Navajo, and Tuzigoot are impor-tant enough to merit preservation as national monuments. The most important of the Indian remains, however, is none of these vestiges of dead civilizations, and not even a ruin, though it could readily be monumentalized if it were one. In the heart of the settlements called "pueblos" along the Rio Grande River in New Mexico, the Taos pueblo was inhabited when the *conquistadores* came riding north from Mexico. It still is, and the Indians today live in the same flat-topped adobe houses four and five stories high their forefathers began.

The Indians who built the Mesa Verde cliff dwellings settled in the area during the first century A.D. They defied heavy snows and cold winters, deriving sustenance from plants and game, clothing from animal skins, shel-ter from rock overhangs, and medicine from various natural sources. In the sixth century they moved to the Mesa tops, where they found a plentiful supply of water and arable soil and began to build permanent rock shel-ters. Gradually through the centuries these Pueblo Indians advanced their culture by re-fining agricultural and industrial skills and the arts, including architecture.

The silent cities of Mesa Verde were oc-cupied for almost 800 years. As I walk through the portions of the park open to view, I can follow the progress in their construction, from pit houses and crude pueblos to great multi-story structures in the sheer rock—towers, terraces, whole towns built of stone blocks in long crannies, huge, arching caves, and atop the Mesa.

At Spruce Tree House, the best-preserved cliff dwelling, I note high walls that still touch the top of the cave and the original roofs still intact. Cliff Palace, largest and most famous of the ruins, built under a high, vaulted cave roof, has more than 200 rooms, of which 23 are kivas, the underground ceremonial chambers for men only. Strategically located Balcony House—built in a choice defensive setting—demonstrates architectural detail and construction skills. Square Tower House, one of the ruins that can be viewed along a 12-mile drive of the canyon rim, has a four-story tower. Long House, opened in 1972 after a major archaeological project on Wetherill Mesa, rivals Cliff Palace in grandeur, with fortresslike dwellings beneath a massive stone canopy. Two other recent additions are Mug House and Step House, also on Wetherill. Up to now only a few of the cliffs have been ex-plored; hundreds of other ruins may never be excavated.

The Indians of Mesa Verde evidently wasted nothing that they drew from nature. They were ingenious people. They introduced cotton along with the true loom. They de-signed a chain of ditches to conserve water atop Chapin Mesa and to eliminate laborious hauling from springs below. In the golden age from A.D. 1100 to 1300, the Classic Pueblo Period, they built handsome stone pueblos, decorating the walls with colored designs of earthen paints. They made beautiful black-on-white pottery without the aid of a wheel, turquoise jewelry, and woven cloth.

Toward the end of the thirteenth century, the Indians left their houses in the cliffs and wandered off gradually, over a long period of time, leaving unfinished the great ceremonial Sun Temple on the surface of the Mesa.

< OVERLEAF: THE GRAND TETONS

 MUG HOUSE AND KIVA

LONG HOUSE ON WETHERILL MESA

Drought probably drove them off, but the true reason remains a mystery. In their wanderings they mingled with other tribes, becoming ancestors of the modern-day Pueblo Indians.

The ruins of Mesa Verde became known only as recently as the late nineteenth century. Then the silent cities were ravaged and ransacked by local men picking up artifacts for sale to museums and collectors in the East and in Europe. This led to passage of the Antiquities Act of 1906, making it a federal offense to remove, injure, damage, or destroy historic objects on federal lands. Mesa Verde National Park was established the same year.

Much of the Mesa Verde is clothed in pinyon-juniper woodlands, a natural life-community hard pressed to survive elsewhere in this part of the country. Besides the mountain and desert plants, the plateau sustains many forms of animal life, including bighorn sheep and wild turkeys, as well as some 150 species of birds.

The gnarled, bent, windblown, hard-bitten two-needle pinyon pine is a despised tree, widely uprooted by a mechanical means called "chaining" and then burned, at great expense of money and energy, to make way for grass for cows. It was not always this way for a tree that lives more than 200 years and guards slopes from erosion. The pinyon nut, really a large wingless seed, has long been a delicacy to birds and other forms of wildlife, as well as to Indians and Easterners, who call it the Indian nut. And pinyon wood was widely used in campfires, burning steadily with an orange-colored flame and a strong fragrance that is warming in itself.

The juniper, a low-growing tree with broken crown, was invaluable to the people of Mesa Verde. They used its bark to weave baskets, bags, sandals, and containers of all sorts. When they developed the pit house, they used juniper poles and sticks, covered with mud, to make low walls and a flat roof over the partly subterranean room.

In more recent times, juniper trees furnished posts for the Mormons when they pioneered the country. The tree was so popular with Utah Mormons, who called it cedar, that they gave its name to Cedar City. The past seems forgotten in the rush to eradicate both pinyon and juniper; we have lost the wisdom of our Indian heritage.

Rocky Mountain National Park

ON A SEPTEMBER DAY THE QUAKING ASPEN ARE BRILLIANT AND VARIED IN COLOR. In some clumps the leaves are still green. Others, I see, have just begun to turn. Then there are those already transformed to a golden hue. The white-trunked aspen (in some places called "popple") grows in many parts of the continent, but its foliage seems to be brighter in Colorado than elsewhere, probably because the thin, dry air of this Rocky Mountain region makes the leaves almost crystalline.

Aspen also grow taller in the southern Rockies, reaching heights of almost 100 feet. Every canyon shows the tree in a different perspective. An isolated clump adorning a rock outcrop looks like a golden crown. Forming streaks of gold down colored cliffs, the trees create a sense of beauty on the scale of sunrise and sunset.

No other collection of mountains south of Canada is as massive or as high as the Colorado Rockies. Of the 50 highest peaks in the United States, including Alaska, more than half are in Colorado. One-third of Rocky Mountain National Park, which is in the north-central part of the state, lies above timberline, and this makes it distinctive, particularly with the contrast between pines, blue spruce, and aspen in the sheltered valleys; the peaks, long ridges, and characteristic glacial U-shaped valley bottoms; and the high alpine tundra.

I look up at the rough and spectacular Front Range, one of the great mountain masses of the world, its highest summits and valley walls mantled in perpetual snows. Winter has already arrived there, or perhaps never left. The national park embraces the heart of the Front Range, which derives its name from being the first wave of the Rockies to rise from the central Great Plains. The valleys are about 8,000 feet above sea level, and within the park are 59 peaks 12,000 feet or higher, including Longs Peak, which at 14,255 feet is the highest of them all.

The peak was named for Colonel Stephen H. Long, who led an expedition to the Rockies in 1820 when he was still a major, apparently the first of the explorers and adventurers venturing into this region after its acquisition through the Louisiana Purchase. He was followed by William Ashley, the fur trader; by the intrepid John C. Frémont, searching for the "great crossing-place" through the Rockies to the Pacific; and by Francis Parkman, the tormented Boston Brahmin devoted to the cult of contact and combat with nature, who left us his breathtaking description of man against nature on the Oregon Trail at mid-century.

FOG-SHROUDED LONGS PEAK

Then settlers arrived with the Colorado Gold Rush of 1859, and an inquisitive Irish nobleman, the Earl of Dunraven, in 1872. The earl fell in love with the country and proceeded to develop a great estate and game preserve, saving many beauty spots from being picked over by prospectors. He entertained Albert Bierstadt, the German-born painter of classic Rocky Mountain landscapes, who captured on canvas the glory of magnificent scenes and left the originals unspoiled.

Enos Mills, naturalist, philosopher, and laureate of the Rockies, was 14 years old when he saw the mountains for the first time. He began a concerted campaign for the establishment of a national park to protect the Colorado Rockies in 1909, traveling and writing extensively to stir up support. His work was rewarded in 1915, when he participated in the dedication ceremonies.

On the trail ascending from Bear Lake I meet late-blooming columbines, the Colorado state flower. The columbine's five white petals form an inner cup in front of five blue sepals—a saucerlike star that dips gracefully in every breeze. The fringed gentian is at its peak when the aspen have turned to gold, a deep purple flower with four petals forming a square column open at the top and flaring outward. These queenly blossoms are found as high as 13,000 feet, surviving blizzards that in a few weeks will sweep the alpine basins with a vengeance.

Pine squirrels, with dark bodies and black tails, chatter most of the way to the 11,000–11,500-foot zone that marks the end of the tree line. Saucy yellow-belly marmots—also known as woodchucks, rockchucks, and whistle-pigs—already showing their fall fat, sit erect and defiant at the doorsteps of their rocky houses, from which they scarcely ever range more than a hundred yards.

Once the Colorado Rockies were a wildlife stronghold, as I dream that one day they will be again. For the present, the grizzlies are gone. Mountain lions are occasionally reported but not seen. These species stand little chance of survival except in the most inaccessible wilderness, beyond the reach of stockmen and "sportsmen." Happily, coyotes are not scarce. While at Moraine Park I have heard their wild yipping song and caught sight of one or two of them hunting up and down the canyons. The tawny-gray coyote merits respect and admiration from the true sportsman. The animal's patience, grace, agility, and speed would do credit to a superbly trained bird dog. In search of small game, particularly rodents, the coyote may stand motionless for long moments, absolutely still like a setter or pointer, then pounce in an arclike, jackknife leap, trapping the prey under its front paws as it comes down.

September is rutting season, the time to hear the resonant and vibrant bugling of the elk. I see their tracks, larger and more blunt than deer tracks, and the telltale pellet droppings, but miss both sight and sound of the handsome wapiti. Elk travel during the rut, but their true migration downward from the high meadows comes when snows fall. Big-

< OVERLEAF: FRONT RANGE

horn sheep, the animals that symbolize Rocky Mountain National Park, also move in winter to lower elevations where food is more readily obtainable. The bighorns always make an impressive sight, moving in a band across lofty rocks, the old rams bearing massive horns that curl a full circle or more.

At Ptarmigan Pass, on the Continental Divide, above glacial lakes, moraines, and sharp valleys carved by vast sheets of moving ice, I walk in the domain where pipits, finches, ptarmigans, and golden eagles fly. Life thins with elevation but doesn't cease. At timberline wind and snow combine to produce gnarled, twisted trees, with branches only on the side towards which the wind is blowing. The Swiss have a special word, *Krummholz*, or "crooked wood," referring to the hardy species that cling tenaciously to life in the high Alps. These are always conifers—limber pine in the Colorado Rockies—for a deciduous tree could not survive in such a harsh environment.

Tiny dwarf plants cluster densely, carrying the banners of life high above timberline. The tundra is an island of Arctic-type vegetation. Moss campion growing in cushiony patches appears here just as it does in the Brooks Range of Alaska and, I suppose, in northern Siberia as well. The mountain climate is severe because of strong winds, dry atmosphere, low soil moisture, and exceptionally strong sunlight. Little wonder that many lichens, mosses, herbs, and shrubs are not only small, low-growing, and compact, but extremely slow-growing as well.

Another day, while driving on the Trail Ridge Road, I contemplate the idea that such mountain environments are fragile, easily susceptible to damage, and slow to recover. The road climbs 5,000 feet on its winding 44-mile course from Estes Park, at the east entrance, to the crest of the Front Range, then descends 4,000 feet to Grand Lake at the west entrance. The road is comfortable and safe all the way;

CHASM FALLS OF THE FALL RIVER

all the motorist needs to do is dress warmly for stops en route in the cold-climate zone.

At Rock Cut, elevation 12,110 feet, near the highest point on the road, I pause to absorb a superlative view. Here is scenic grandeur of the highest order: to the northeast, the Mummy Range, a tumbled mountain mass including some of the park's loftiest peaks; to the south, Longs Peak, its square granite head rising above its 12,000-foot and 13,000-foot neighbors; to the west, gentler slopes, dotted with streams and lakes. Walking the trail from the overlook, I note tiny plants matted, flower stalks broken by human trampling. Plainly, walking on tundra can be destructive—not only where people park their cars, but wherever the trails lead.

The steep slopes, the lack of trees whose roots stabilize the soil, and the thinness of the soil combine to favor conditions for easy erosion. In the 1960s Dr. Bettie Willard undertook ecological studies of the alpine vegetation in the national park and recorded the effects of intensive human use. She found areas where, after four decades of trampling in the short summer, all plants were gone, except the few protected by large boulders, and where five inches of topsoil were gone too, leaving a bare mineral soil surface. It was estimated that a minimum of 500 years would be necessary to restore the tundra ecosystem.

We need to walk lightly, *more* lightly, in the high places; to admire and respect, with restraint, so that the tundra may restore itself. In the history of the earth, 500 years is not that long.

SUNRISE OVER SPRAGUE LAKE

Grand Teton National Park

BOLD SOARING SUMMITS RISE FROM THE EARTH WITHOUT FOOTHILLS. MY FIRST VIEW OF the Tetons years ago was from the west side, driving north from Pocatello, Idaho. I saw these snow-crested spires parading against the clear Wyoming sky, so dramatic a spectacle that I could scarcely concentrate on driving and pulled off the road to stare in wonder. Even now, many visits later, I never fail to get the same feeling. From whatever angle I approach, the cluster of huge peaks dominates the scene. From within the park, on the east side, they spread their images, with cirques, horns, knife-edged ridges, headlong slopes, and pinnacles, across the waters of Jenny Lake, Lake Solitude, and Jackson Lake. There is absolutely no escaping the scene.

The Tetons are a great block of the earth's crust almost 40 miles long, a "fault-block" mountain range thrust upward along a fault, or crack, in the surface. Later the mountains were sculpted by wind, water, frost, and glaciation, but the durable granite rocks have resisted erosion much more than the lava plateaus of nearby Yellowstone. From the floor of the valley, 6,500 feet high, the Grand Teton rises to an elevation of 13,770 feet above sea level—substantially more than a mile above the plain.

The valley, called Jackson Hole, with its sagebrush flats, forests, rivers, lakes, and marshlands, is one of the legendary corners of Wyoming, a place that until recently knew little of cities or city ways. It wasn't many years ago that the Wort Hotel was about the only place to stay in the cow town of Jackson at the foot of the valley. Now Jackson is one of those booming resort colonies where private land is worth more as real estate than as cow pasture, and most open space to be saved is already public land.

Indians passed through Jackson Hole in pursuit of the elk on which they depended for food. Then came the traders and trappers,

LAKE SOLITUDE

adventurous mountain men such as Jim Bridger, William Sublette, David Jackson, and Jedediah Smith who blazed trails, located water and grass, and named the lakes and rivers, while hunting buffalo, elk, antelope, and deer and trapping beaver. Homesteaders found this high country too cold and barren for farming and left it largely to cattlemen.

Grand Teton National Park was established in 1929, but there wasn't much of it at first; it covered only the east side of the range and very little of the lowland that was needed for winter elk range. John D. Rockefeller, Jr., benefactor of parks, who had been to Yellowstone—which borders Grand Teton on the north—was encouraged by national park officials to take an interest in the Teton country. Through a dummy corporation, the Snake River Land Company, he purchased more than 35,000 acres in the Jackson Hole Basin and presented it to the government. This land was set aside as Jackson Hole National Monument over the opposition of stockmen, hunters, dude ranchers, and the Forest Service, which had been the dominant federal agency in the area. Most of the monument became a part of the national park in 1950; the remainder was absorbed in the National Elk Refuge. I recall meeting Clifford Hansen at the opening of the Rockefeller-built Jackson Lake Lodge in 1956. He was one of Jackson Hole's prominent stockmen and later governor of Wyoming and U.S. senator. "For years," he told me, "I fought these people and now I'm on their board of directors. I can't believe I'm here."

Much of Jackson Hole has reverted to nature, as it should within a national park. Being a preservationist, I search for the ultimate and find instead the flaws. There are too many miles of main-stem highway, too many head of privately owned cattle still grazing in the park. There is an airport that should have been moved out years ago and that now is programmed for jet transport service—I can't think of anything less compatible with the spirit and purpose of the Grand Tetons. And Rockefeller, despite his best intentions, was a landscaper rather than a champion of wild nature. I doubt that he had anyone to tell him forcefully when he was wrong. So he placed his large hotel where it's right for viewing the scenery through the picture windows but wrong for the protection of ecosystems. It would never have passed an environmental impact statement.

I enjoy floating down the Snake River with Vern Huser, who used to teach school in Jackson and returns summers from Salt Lake City to work as a boatman and guide in the park. He knows the places in the bottom woodlands and marshes where eagles nest, moose browse, and beavers build their lodges. Vern has made many trips over the same course, but because he loves this wild, winding river and the mountains above it, many is never enough.

The Snake is the second-longest river in the Northwest. It rises here in western Wyoming, motherland of glorious rivers—including the Green (which becomes the main stem of the Colorado), the Madison and Gallatin forks of the Missouri, and the Yellowstone—to begin its thousand-mile journey to merge with the Columbia.

After joining the waters of little streams from high lakes and forests in the Teton and Yellowstone country, the Snake flows through the beautiful forested canyon south of Jackson, then winds across the sagebrush plains of southern Idaho before turning sharply north. William Clark named it the Lewis River, after Meriwether Lewis, his intrepid co-captain in the Lewis and Clark expedition, but others insisted on using the Indian name of *Shoshoneah*, which translates into English as "Snake," and Snake it is. In recent years the Snake has been plugged by 12 major dams of varying sizes, shapes, and purposes, so the stretch in the Tetons is one of the last that remain untamed and unspoiled, approaching the natural conditions in which man found the river.

From the sagebrush valley at the south end of Leigh Lake I climb across glacial moraines cloaked in lodgepole pine into the subalpine zone of fir and spruce. As I enter the heart of the range, the Tetons become a network of rock gardens on cliffs and ledges, filled with waterfalls and wild flowers. Paintbrush Canyon is bordered, naturally, with huge clumps of bright red-orange paintbrush, blue columbine, mountain gentian, and other flowers. Above the cliffs and peaks birds of prey soar and wheel on rising air currents—sparrow hawks and prairie falcons, with golden eagles even higher still. For a little while I share with them vistas of the clear lakes, the Snake River flowing through sagebrush meadows and forest, the Gros Ventre Range on the east and south, the high plateaus of Yellowstone to the north, and the mighty Tetons. The mountains change in appearance with the seasons and with the hours of the day; they are never twice the same, even through the same eyes.

Yellowstone National Park

I LOVE YELLOWSTONE AS THE FIRST NATIONAL PARK, THE PLACE WHERE THE IDEA OF NATURE RE-serves, though born earlier, was applied in practice, establishing the principle that land is more than a commodity to buy and sell, and holds implicit value in its own right to an entire nation.

I love to be in Yellowstone because it is the largest national park, embracing vast distances of sagebrush desert, open meadow, and high forest, a complex of resources that are not "used" for the benefit of man in the ordinary sense. Trees are allowed to die and decompose, to the forester's despair. Minerals lie undisturbed in rocky places. Grasses are for wild animals rather than for domestic livestock —all of which enables Yellowstone to endure as the nation's largest wildlife sanctuary.

Early explorers were mystified and spellbound by Yellowstone's freaks of nature, the 10,000 hot water geysers, fumaroles, terraces, hot springs, and bubbling mud pots that make it the most extensive thermal area on earth. It was these and other geological phenomena— notably the Grand Canyon of the Yellowstone River, where brawling waters rush through twisting rock walls, and beautiful Yellowstone Lake, the largest body of water in North America at so high an elevation (some 138 square miles at 7,731 feet)—that led to its designation as a national park. Yellowstone comprises 2,219,823 acres largely free of man's influence, and that, today, is a quality equally unique. More than 2 million of the total acreage is in Wyoming, the remainder overlaps into Montana and Idaho.

John Colter, who left the Lewis and Clark expedition in 1806 to become a trapper and free-lance explorer, is believed to have been the first white man to see and report on this country. His sober relation of the wonders he saw was received as a monumental exercise in yarn-spinning; "Colter's Hell" became a legend. Then Jim Bridger, rawboned, gray-eyed "Old Gabe," followed, adding his tales about the cliff of black glass, the spouting hot springs, and the belching sulfurous steam,

MINERVA TERRACE AT MAMMOTH HOT SPRINGS

which were put down as "Jim Bridger's lies."

Expeditions followed, gradually building a picture of the "Yellow Rock" country. One group that came to verify the frontier stories set out from Fort Ellis, Montana, on August 21, 1870, led by Henry D. Washburn, surveyor general of Montana, and Nathaniel Pitt Langford, with Lieutenant Gustavus C. Doane commanding a small military escort. Within a month they covered an amazing amount of ground, mapping known wonders, discovering more, and giving names to many of the features, including Old Faithful.

According to accounts, one September evening around a campfire at the junction of the Firehole and Gibbon rivers, the members of the party discussed what to do with the wonderland they had explored. Judge Cornelius Hedges suggested—and the others agreed—that they pass up the possibility of profitable speculation and work instead on getting the area set apart and held by the government. And work they did, especially Langford, who carried the crusade to the East, lecturing in the cities and talking with federal officials. Both he and Hedges wrote articles describing the marvels of Yellowstone and stressing the importance of protecting the area for the enjoyment of all the people. It was a revolutionary idea, yet their enthusiasm led to an official scientific expedition the following year. The endorsement for a federal preserve by Ferdinand V. Hayden, the leader of the Geological Survey, was supported by a superb set of photographs taken by William H. Jackson, plainly showing that the scouts and trappers and the Washburn party weren't exaggerating. The now-renowned paintings of Thomas Moran, another member of the expedition, also helped, and in 1872 Yellowstone National Park was established by Congressional action. Langford was named superintendent.

The protection of this vast wilderness holds up in the passage of time as a monumental act of idealism by an entire nation. The original design was to insure public ownership of a spectacular scenic resource. Then other values emerged. The last significant herd of bison found refuge in the park. Yellowstone held the largest elk herds in the United States, and beaver were still common in its streams and brooks, while outside its boundaries these species had been nearly exterminated or greatly reduced in numbers. Within a few years the demonstrated value of Yellowstone led to establishment of forest reservations to protect watershed and timber resources, as well as wildlife, then to national wildlife refuges, and ultimately to national parks and comparable reserves throughout the world.

In June, 1964, I am on a memorable visit to Yellowstone, showing the park to my own family. One night we are quartered at the Old Faithful Inn, the sprawling gingerbread wooden masterwork of 1903. We have stood during the day at the edge of the great geyser, the emblem of the park, that has never missed an eruption in more than 80 years of observation—not quite on the hour, but at intervals averaging about 65 minutes. Our rooms face Old Faithful, and throughout the night I find myself awakening to watch it. Almost every time my wife is already sitting up in her bed, and so are the two children in the next room. All of us are spellbound, absorbing the sequence; first a little hot water and steam well forth from the top of the cone, then fall back; next the water gushes a little higher, and increasing in volume finally soaring to about 150 feet, with billowing steam far above, a snowy haze outlined against forest and sky—more than 10,000 gallons of water roaring in a spectacle lasting some four minutes.

We tour the geysers, which are clustered in well-defined "basins" and as varied as they are numerous. Some go off at fairly regular inter-vals. Large ones send streams 200 feet into the air; small ones, spouts of only a few feet in height. I suggest that we bypass a basin; after all, we've seen plenty already. "But each is different," protests my 12-year-old son, and of course he's right. Norris Basin is filled with exciting bubbling springs and geysers, including Steamboat, the most powerful geyser in the park. Upper, Midway, and Lower basins contain wonderlands of scalding water and superheated steam, reflecting tremendous heat inside the earth.

These jets of hot water propelled by explosive forces are found at only three places—New Zealand, Iceland, and Yellowstone. Of the 10,000 "hot water volcanoes" in the national park, more than 200 are geysers. They are caused when cold waters trickling downward strike vapors rising from superhot magmas. The waters boil upward, emerging at the surface as steam. The volcanic upheavals of long ago left the landscape in a smoking jumble that simply has not cooled. The hot springs show that active lava is not far below, and the explosive eruptions, that the violence is not finished.

TOWER FALLS

OLD FAITHFUL

These phenomena are scattered throughout the park. At Mammoth Hot Springs, huge terraces have been formed on the side of Terrace Mountain (at the rate of six inches to a foot a year) by lime emitted in solution from hot springs hundreds of feet below and deposited in the form of travertine. At Black Sand Basin, vivid orange and yellow colors trace colonies of microscopic organisms—diatoms and algae —growing at the limits of life in the hot springs. Grand Prismatic Spring, Yellowstone's largest hot spring, also is ringed with algal color, contrasting with the brilliant blue of the pool. The Morning Glory Pool is named for its fancied resemblance to the color and corolla of the morning glory flower.

Near Old Faithful my family and I walk along the Firehole River, the stream that Jim Bridger said "gets hot on the bottom." But the heat actually derives from the drainage of thermal features near the riverbanks and from hot springs in the bed, not from friction of water on the rock, as some believed. Then we pause to watch the lovely Firehole Cascades, a stretch of white water rushing on its way between banks of grass and wild flowers against a dark evergreen forest and black lava rock.

Most such features are along the Grand Loop, designed in an earlier day for easy sightseeing. But there are others beyond the road— secluded pools of boiling water, simmering creeks, and steam eruptions. From road's end at Lone Star Geyser, a seven-mile trail strewn with obsidian (a black volcanic glass) leads to Shoshone Geyser Basin, a fantastic thermal area that takes hours to explore.

Every part of Yellowstone is alive and changing, as part of the grand cycle of nature beyond man's control or full comprehension. Water and wind cut canyons and erode exposed rock, crumbling stone into soil. Thermal features dissolve underground rock with heat and acid, then bring it up to deposit on the surface. And there are earthquakes.

This is earthquake country. In 1960 I am in Yellowstone to learn the cause and effect of the Hebgen quake of the year before, when half a mountain in Gallatin National Forest, near the northwest corner of the park, collapsed into the valley below. Montana earthquakes are the result of stresses building up over long periods between huge masses of subterranean rock. Dr. Irving Witkind of the Geological Survey, who was near the scene when it happened, teaches me how to identify the remnants of overturned rock folds forming the ridges along Route 287, and how to look for signs of faults, the schisms in the rocks; of thrust faulting, the thrusting of one rock mass

atop another; and of fault scarps, fresh clifflike breaks in the earth.

With the Hebgen quake, the whole plumbing of the earth went haywire. Big springs became bigger, discharging large amounts of fine sediment and turning the water in streams a blotchy and cloudy brown. New springs spouted, while other springs and wells were shut off. In Yellowstone, geysers exploded violently in reaction to the quake. Some erupted after years of quiet, while others ran dry.

"The intriguing thing," observes Dr. Witkind with complete assurance, "was that stresses were released along old existing breaks. It confirmed the picture we had discerned. In fact, I had drawn lines on a map of a series of old fault scarps." On my notepaper he sketches several red lines to indicate the new break. "When the earthquake hit, it repeated the patterns of history."

Yellowstone is surrounded by a series of great ranges of the Rockies—the Absaroka along the east, the Gallatin on the west, the Grand Tetons to the south—but the park itself is essentially a high, rolling plateau, or series of plateaus. The scenery is surprisingly gentle. Even mountains more than 11,000 feet above sea level do not appear high because they rise from elevations of almost 8,000 feet.

The Grand Canyon of the Yellowstone River thus comes as a surprise, a breathtaking spectacle from any vantage point along its

twisting 24-mile course. At Artist Point I watch the thundering Lower Falls plunging 308 feet (equal to two Niagaras) into the foaming water below. And at Inspiration Point, which juts almost into the center of the canyon, I study the walls. The dominant color is yellow, ranging from pale lemon to bright orange in the shade, but red, brown, pink, and white add to the profusion, reflecting the mineral compounds in the rock. This too will change with the continual crumbling of the banks.

Bear, moose, elk, bison, bighorn sheep, deer, antelope, wolves, coyotes, and smaller animals roam at will. Or perhaps I should say almost at will. Black bears are common along the Grand Loop, where they beg for food from misguided summer visitors who persist in treating bears as though they were some form of house pet. Once I saw a father try to place a small child on the back of a bear for a posed photograph. Every summer, despite warnings, many people are bitten or clawed. The "rogue bears," behaving only in their own fashion, are trapped and moved. Should one return to cause more trouble, it is dispatched by rangers to bear heaven. Even those bears that make it through the tourist summer are ill equipped for the harsh reality of feeding themselves during the winter.

Grizzlies are believed to number about 250 in the park, the most important refuge left to them anywhere in the United States outside of

Alaska. It is sometimes stated that the developed areas cover only 5 percent of Yellowstone, leaving the remainder for wildlife, but grizzlies don't use the 95 percent. They have their favored locations, concentrated on the Central and Mirror plateaus and in the Gallatin Range, where they find food and cover, though this is apt to change from time to time. For years they were fed at garbage dumps to attract visitors, inside the park and at West Yellowstone. That practice, happily, has been terminated; the condition of the grizzly bears as an endangered species requires constant watching, but they appear to be adjusting to a more natural environment.

In late afternoon a lone trumpeter swan pokes its solid black bill into the tall grasses and reeds of the placid Madison River in search of food. Presently the bird stretches its snow-white wings, seven feet from tip to tip, squawks its distinctive, low-pitched resonant *beep*, and glides gracefully upstream.

The trumpeter swan, Yellowstone's largest waterfowl, once bred over a vast area of the continent, as far south as Indiana, Missouri,

and Nebraska, and wintered in southern California and on the Gulf Coast. Then most of its range was preempted for settlement and development. Its great size made it an easy target for shooters, and the swan was pressed to the brink of extinction. In 1932 a count showed less than 70 in the entire country. Under protection, the bird has made a comeback, increasing by the mid-1970s to an estimated total of more than 4,000. There are flocks in wild parts of northern Canada, but the sanctuaries of Yellowstone and Red Rocks Waterfowl Refuge in southwestern Montana are essential to its survival.

The trumpeter swan is only one of the more than 200 species of birds in the park. One day, with the park superintendent and a ranger I cruise on patrol into the South Arm and Southeast Arm of Yellowstone Lake, a marvelous natural body of blue water 300 feet deep, fed by snow stored in the forests above it. No roads reach the arms and no powerboats are permitted, though there are several campgrounds located along the shores.

Deep in the Southeast Arm, we near the

Molly Islands—but not too near, since these islands provide breeding grounds for the endangered white pelican, as well as for gulls, cormorants, and terns. With binoculars I not only spot a pelican roost, but also catch sight of an adult, a huge white-and-black bird, diving for a fish, which it scoops up in its basket-like bill and then carries home.

On the lakes, streams, sloughs, and backwaters, I find one species or another: bald eagles, ospreys, sandhill cranes, great blue herons, kingfishers—and mammals too—dependent on fish for a major portion of their diet. Today the fish are protected to a certain extent, with parts of specified lakes and rivers closed to anglers, particularly during the spawning season. In addition, fishermen are being asked to release the trout they catch. Small steps—but in the right direction.

On one of the park's entrance gates a sign reads: "For the benefit and enjoyment of the people." It's the wildlife, from least to largest, that sets Yellowstone apart and enhances the substantial benefit and enjoyment.

LODGEPOLE PINE FOREST

Glacier National Park

HIKING TOWARD TIMBERLINE, I CAN SEE THE SHIMMERING CASCADES OF GLACIER NA-tional Park dropping thousands of feet from high snowfields. Far above, the rocky rampart called the Garden Wall blocks out the sky for miles. Loose shale and a strong wind make footing difficult, and the steepest part, a climb of about 1,500 feet in less than a mile, is still ahead.

There are times when I wonder why I dare to follow trails made for younger people. Getting around on a horse is a lot easier, and I've done plenty of riding in the Western mountains; but now I take into consideration that a horse does more damage on the trail than a hiker, and there's less satisfaction in the easy way. I look across snow-topped mountains carved like matterhorns, pyramids, and Mayan temples and down at great chasms yawning below—the embodiment of the northern Rockies, a world of enormous ridges and valleys. I feel as though I belong for this moment to something large and important. Let arthritis wait and the young take care of themselves.

The cool Montana slopes are covered with flowering species. Bear grass is by all odds the most prominent and abundant, with creamy white flowers atop a tall stalk. Also known as Indian basket grass or squaw grass, it is a lily rather than a grass. Obviously the native people gave this plant its common name and found it useful. On the higher slopes, above the forests of lodgepole pine, little forget-me-nots and shooting stars grow in thin soils surrounded by patches of snow and ice that will not melt this year.

Fat and sassy marmots frolic in the rock piles. I hear the shrill, high notes of pikas, or coneys, the furry rock rabbit that is more likely to be heard than seen. The surrounding cliffs are "mountain goat walls," and presently my hope for a glimpse of these amazing climbers is rewarded. Across the valley on Grinnell Point I spot a sole nanny and her kid, graceful and surefooted, in their whitish-yellow coats. The kid follows mother closely but is self-possessed, undaunted by heights or cliffs.

The mountain goat resembles the domestic goat in form but is actually an antelope, re-lated to the European chamois. This scene in Glacier calls to mind my visit to the Vanoise National Park in the French Alps, where I watched in fascination a herd of *bouquetin*, the rare alpine ibex, moving along steep, rugged slopes. For years the ibex had been slaughtered by hunters while passing from the Gran Paradiso refuge in bordering Italy into the Vanoise through the Col de l'Iseran. So the national park was established on the French side to save this vanishing species. Fortunately, in our country the mountain goat is inaccessible for most hunters, and its head doesn't make much of an adornment for the trophy wall.

On the trail ascending from Many Glacier Valley I had passed a number of youthful hikers. They were bear-conscious and wary, often shaking a cowbell or toting a can with a few rocks in it to stir up a noise, mindful that a grizzly is apt to charge when startled, but likely to move elsewhere when forewarned that humans are approaching. Dr. George Ruhle, who served for many years as park naturalist, learned that grizzlies are not unduly disturbed by the human voice, so whenever he encountered one of the big bears he would talk to it continuously as a gesture of peace and good faith—a valid technique, but one re-quiring steady nerves, as well as experience in the wilds.

Glacier National Park is one of the last strongholds of the grizzly bear, God's own creature. The grizzly runs like the wind, fishes better with bare teeth than any man with rod and reel, and roars like distant thunder. Once about 1½ million grizzlies roamed across the West. Now there are fewer than a thousand in the United States south of Alaska, concen-trated in the wild, rugged mountain country of the national forests and national parks of the northern Rockies. Grizzly country in the for-ests has been seriously disrupted in recent years by roads, logging, use of chemical poi-sons, and policies favoring livestock grazing, so that preservation of natural conditions in Glacier and Yellowstone is essential to the fu-ture of the grizzly bear.

Before the turn of the century grizzlies were trapped in the Glacier country for their furry hides. Hundreds of elk, moose, sheep, goats, and deer were slaughtered each year so their carcasses could be used for bear bait. Es-tablishment of the park in 1910 provided sanc-tuary to these species, as well as the mountain lion, coyote, lynx, hawk, eagle, and the rest.

How secure, really, is a sanctuary of wild-life with trails, roads, and camps for human use and enjoyment? In 1967, two campers in Glacier were pulled from sleeping bags by grizzly bears, dragged off into the woods, and

WATER-CARVED ROCK IN McDONALD CANYON

killed. Nine years later another Glacier visitor died after being mauled by a grizzly. Following each of these tragic events two bears were killed by park rangers. I was in the park after both incidents and reviewed the circumstances closely. The grizzlies had not invaded a populated area; they were in their own territory. Though I feel safer on a park trail than on a downtown city street, I recognize that there is always the risk of confrontation in bear country—the higher the use of an area, the higher the risk. Nevertheless, the national parks are not for men alone; they are equally for the native American animals that were in these areas first. This is at the heart of the concept of national parks.

The Continental Divide bisects the park for its entire length, from north to south. Astride the Divide at Swiftcurrent Pass, 4,900 feet above Many Glacier Valley, I can see the expansive evidence of huge Ice Age glaciers. Once they covered all but the highest peaks; then they gouged the valleys, scooped out hundreds of lakes that now sparkle like jewels, and sliced mountains into stark forms. One section of the Divide was sheared into a long thin cliff, named the Garden Wall for the fields of pink monkey flowers that bloom below it. About 50 alpine glaciers are still nestled among the higher peaks, most of them now hardly more than large snow patches in the shadows of ice-carved valleys.

Iceberg Lake, more than a thousand feet below me, is one of those glacial-carved beauties, filling the floor of a cirque and enclosed on three sides by steep vertical walls. Closer at hand, a half dozen waterfalls tumble from Swiftcurrent Glacier, a thin strip of ice in the broad basin above the summit of Swiftcurrent Mountain. And south along the Garden Wall, in a vast rocky cradle, lies Grinnell Glacier, consisting of two sectors of snowfields draping peaks and slopes. Fifty years ago it formed a single continuous ice mass. The main part of the glacier may be gone, but the floor beneath it shows the grooving and polishing caused by the rocks it once held in a viselike grip.

MOUNT JACKSON

I arrive at the Granite Park Chalets, perched on the rim of a lava ledge. These rustic quarters were designed in the early days of the park, before the advent of lightweight backpacking gear, to furnish minimum shelter and hot meals. The chalets overlook scores of tumbling waterfalls, lakes, and silvery streams. To the north lies Mount Cleveland, 10,448 feet, the highest peak in the park, just below the Canadian border and Waterton Lakes National Park.

Glacier is unique among the national parks in that officially it is more than one nation's park. Together Glacier, in northwestern Montana, and Waterton Lakes, in southwestern Alberta, form Waterton-Glacier International Peace Park. The two were joined in 1932, as a symbol of the good will between Canada and the United States.

One would like to believe that in such a vast arena nature would be secure, that Waterton Lake (which lies in both countries), Lake McDonald, and St. Mary Lake, known throughout the world, and the lustrous forests around them would be safe forever. Yet within the past few years fluoride pollutants from mineral smelters outside Glacier have been detected in the park's ecosystem, and now the clear streams are endangered by proposed mining in the upper Flathead Valley. To save a priceless fragment like Glacier National Park, even though designated for preservation by law, is no easy task. It demands continual vigilance.

Fortunately, there are sources of inspiration and of hope. At Granite Park I absorb the golden glow of sunset over the sharp peaks and ridges. The northern Rockies may have their crashing summer storms and frigid winters with hip-deep snows, but for sheer God-given glory this is the place. And in the still of night, while watching the northern lights play throughout the sky from rim to rim, I know that the treasure in our care must endure.

Then I think of George Bird Grinnell, the man most responsible for establishing Glacier National Park, whose name has been given to a glacier, mountain, waterfall, point, and lake, and to the reddish rock that colors many formations.

Born in New York to well-to-do parents, Grinnell received his first formal education, and everlasting love of nature, from the widow of John J. Audubon. Following his graduation from Yale, where he earned his Ph.D., he made the first of many trips to the West. He became a friend and champion of the Indians, emerging as a scholar on the Shawnee, Blackfeet, Cheyenne, and Pawnee. Then, as the editor and publisher of *Forest and Stream Magazine*,

ICEBERG LAKE

REYNOLDS AND HEAVY RUNNER MOUNTAINS

he hunted, fished, climbed mountains, explored glaciers, and luxuriated amid the mountain scenery and wildlife. He was also an ornithologist, and in 1886 he founded the first Audubon society.

Once, while hunting sheep with the Indians in the Glacier country, he spotted a handsome animal and killed it with a single shot at about 150 yards, whereupon his famous sidekick J. W. ("Appekunny") Schultz proudly proclaimed that the mountain would henceforth be known as Singleshot in honor of the achievement. And so it is.

With his friend Theodore Roosevelt, Grinnell organized the Boone and Crockett Club, an organization of elite big-game hunters who worked to protect and perpetuate the species. He saw national parks as refuges for bison and other threatened big game and led the fight for tough laws to prohibit all shooting in the parks. In time he lost his own interest in killing and concentrated his efforts on preservation.

The establishment of Glacier National Park—"The Crown of the Continent," as he called it—was his greatest victory. When President Calvin Coolidge presented the Roosevelt Memorial Medal to Grinnell in 1925, he declared: "Few have done as much as you, and none has done more to preserve vast areas of picturesque wilderness for the eyes of posterity in the simple majesty in which you and your fellow pioneers first beheld them."

What a marvelous encomium, and a model to follow.

BEARHEAD MOUNTAIN AND HIDDEN LAKE

Theodore Roosevelt National Park

THE LITTLE MALTESE CROSS RANCH CABIN WITH LOW SLOPING ROOF SEEMS AT FIRST AN UNlikely abode for an Eastern young man of breeding. But not if you have followed the trail of Theodore Roosevelt, both before and after he came to the Little Missouri Badlands of North Dakota. It all fits together in the shaping of Roosevelt's singular personality and his lasting influence.

From the outside the cabin, or ranch house, which now sits adjacent to the park Visitor Center, looks extremely modest. The side and end walls were made of railroad ties and pilings. On my visit I learn that Roosevelt had removed the original high-pitched roof and upper half-story, then had covered the roof with dirt and the red bricklike rock called "scoria," a practice common at the time. Inside, however, the place doesn't look bad at all. Luxury features include the floor and partitions that divide the cabin into three rooms, which many ranch houses just didn't have. Roosevelt actually had a bedroom all his own, but then he was the boss.

What brought him here? In the fall of 1883, when he was not yet 25 (but already three years out of Harvard), Roosevelt came west to hunt buffalo and other big game, as many affluent Easterners were doing. But there

was a deeper motivation. In conquering his childhood physical frailty, Roosevelt had developed a passion for sport, combined with history, nature, and writing. While in the Badlands he witnessed the passing of one of the last frontiers. "Up to 1880," he wrote later, "the country through which the Little Missouri flows remained as wild and almost as unknown as it was when old explorers and fur traders crossed it in the early part of the century." Theodore Roosevelt was a part of history, as well as the historian.

In 1884, dejected by family tragedies (his mother and young wife had died on the same day) and political reverses in New York, Roosevelt chose a full-time ranching career on the unfenced public lands. First he and partners purchased the Maltese Cross Ranch. Then he established a second ranch, the Elkhorn, about 35 miles north of the frontier settlement of Medora, and built a herd that may once have numbered as many as 5,000 head.

His life on the Badlands was filled with what he called "perfect freedom." As he described it at the time, "There are few sensations I prefer to that of galloping over these rolling limitless prairies, rifle in hand, or winding my way among the barren, fantastic and grimly picturesque deserts of the so-called Bad Lands."

From the Visitor Center I explore the land Roosevelt loved, now a national park in memorial to him. In the South Unit, from Painted Canyon Overlook I see a panoramic view of the buttes and bluffs, the mesas, washes, and sharply eroded valleys. Contrasting bands of light and dark are reminders of the ancient past when broad rivers deposited thick layers of sediment on a plain. In some places trace amounts of iron-rich minerals stain the rocks shades of yellow and buff, while darker grays and browns predominate on higher plateaus. It's fascinating to study the cross-bedded sandstone, with fine particles arranged in a graceful pattern bent like a bow. At Scoria Point, massive bluffs are capped with red scoria, where a vein of lignite burned and baked sand and clay into the natural brick. Thick black layers of lignite are reminders of buried swampy forests transformed into seams of low-grade coal.

On the North Unit I find breathtaking views of bluish bentonitic clay and weird erosional patterns carved by the restless Little Missouri. Where a huge section of the bluff has slipped to the valley floor, bands of color once horizontal are now perched at almost every conceivable angle.

"Grand, dismal and majestic" are the words used to describe the region by General

CLAY FORMS

ARTWORK OF EROSION

CLAY CANYONS IN LITTLE MISSOURI RIVER COUNTRY

Alfred Sully following his campaign against the Sioux in 1864. Supposedly he said the Badlands looked like "hell with the fires out." During the autumn and winter of 1875–76 Sitting Bull led a large encampment, about ten miles from Roosevelt's Elkhorn Ranch, then Lieutenant Colonel George A. Custer and his troops passed through in search of the Sioux en route to their fateful encounter at the Little Bighorn in Montana.

With the Indian wars of the 1870s, the power of the Sioux as lords of the plains was broken. Ranchers arrived to stock cattle on the rangeland where millions of buffalo had roamed. Among them were Easterners like Theodore Roosevelt and wealthy Europeans like the romantic Marquis de Mores, who planned to raise cattle, slaughter and dress them locally, then ship the beef east in refrigerator cars. At Medora, the town he established, I visit his chateau, with its sweeping view of town, river, and Badlands.

The grandest dreams and schemes came to naught. Planless overgrazing on the unfenced open plains reduced the productivity of the grasslands. Then in the bitter winter of 1886–87 cattle perished by the thousands and the bubble was burst. Roosevelt lost more money than he made in ranching and turned his attention to other interests. Even as he rose in politics, however, lessons he learned on the Badlands stayed with him. As a sportsman he helped organize the Boone and Crockett Club, dedicated to preservation of America's big game. One of his first acts on becoming president was to urge the establishment of a new herd of buffalo in Yellowstone National Park so they would never become extinct.

Proposals to honor Roosevelt by creating a national park in the Badlands were advanced by local citizens soon after his death in 1919. A national memorial park of some 70,000 acres (the only one of its kind in the National Park System) was established by Congress in 1947; then it was reclassified as a national park in 1978.

Portions of the park even now are still isolated and untamed. The Badlands are tough, defiant of conquest. Native short grasses are the dominant cover, where there is cover at all (in contrast to the mixed grasses of the South Dakota Badlands). The short grasses have a natural beauty all their own. In spring the pale, lovely pasqueflower appears first, joined presently by blue penstemon, phlox, and violets, and by the evening star that blooms only during hours of darkness. Summer days are long this far north, but the season is short. Autumn may be the best time of year, when frosts slowly cure the grasses to rich, tawny gold and crown the broad-leaved trees and shrubs with yellow and red. Aloft, sandhill cranes and geese wing their way south from the Canadian prairies. I can hardly imagine a more fitting living memorial to Theodore Roosevelt.

Badlands National Park

EVENING SHADOWS ADVANCE ACROSS THE BADLANDS WILDERNESS. THE PASTEL BLUES, PINKS, greens, and bands of tan engraved in the ridges, low hills, and cliffs yield to oncoming grays and blacks in bolder, broader tones. In the rhythmic process of day to night, the forms change, too. What had seemed only minutes ago like the Pyramids of Egypt or the Wall of China have become Inca temples, at least in my fantasy.

Nighttime in Sage Creek Basin is meant for fantasy. In the moonlight black shadows dance across ridges and spires. Two friends and I are alone in the heart of rolling prairie, with grassy hills and wooded draws interspersed with the weird formations designated as "Badlands." It's a marvelous night for sleeping out, but not much for sleeping, not with the chance to listen to coyotes howl and the breeze whistle through the buttes, and to watch the procession of stars, planets, nebulas, and constellations across the clear heavens.

Throughout the night I find myself observing the landscape around me. This portion of western South Dakota is like some strange planet, a moonscape of spires, towers, and pinnacles, an endless array of sudden, unexpected shapes. The Badlands Wall, as it's called, stretches more than 70 miles across the prairie, west to east, made up of soft sedimentary materials being continually sculpted by wind and rain, water and frost, into new forms.

The land where we hike and camp once was part of a shallow inland sea. Then, about 60 million years ago, the Rockies and Black Hills pushed up through the earth's crust. A whole part of the continent rose, leaving the sea bottom a plain of mud before it dried out and became grassland. Now erosion uncovers the past: skeletons of giant reptiles and fish from the ancient Cretaceous sea, and skeletons of Oligocene saber-toothed cats, three-toed horses, small camels, and rhinoceros-like animals—the fossilized remains of hundreds of extinct creatures exhumed from their ancient tombs of mud and clay.

During days in the national park my companions and I hike across the Badlands and the mixed-grass prairie, in which we identify and examine blue grama, needle and thread, western wheatgrass, buffalo grass, and side oats grama, the dominant species among many kinds of grasses. It strikes me as odd that while visitors focus on wildlife, they generously overlook the plants upon which animals depend. Here on the Great Plains the numbers and varieties of wildlife once were among the most plentiful on earth, rivaling the legendary herds of Africa, precisely because the seas of grass furnished an endless food supply.

In the Sage Creek Wilderness we watch (from a respectable distance) a protected remnant herd of about 300 bison following patterns of their forefathers, though their migration routes are now restricted. Moving in vast herds, sometimes covering 50 square miles, the bison of the past would consume thousands of tons of grass in a single day without destroying it. They would trample the grass, but the excrement of these huge beasts, which weighed up to 3,000 pounds each, served as natural fertilizer. Gophers and ground squirrels by their burrowing invited penetration of air and moisture, while wolves and coyotes

ERODED LANDSCAPE

"SCULPTED" BUTTES IN CEDAR PASS

controlled the buffalo numbers. Thus the community of plants and animals maintained a complementary balance.

Then there were the native people. The Sioux, or Lakota, were as nomadic as the bison, following the herds across the plains. When the bison were decimated during the great hunts between 1830 and 1880, the glorious days of the Sioux passed with them. The park, indeed, is deep in the Sioux heartland. In the winter of 1890, the fateful year of the Wounded Knee Massacre, a band of more than a thousand Indians fled to these Badlands for refuge, dancing the Ghost Dance atop the Stronghold Table, hoping to invoke the spirits to end the reservation life and restore their freedom to roam. Curiously, one of the first advocates of the national park idea, the nineteenth-century artist George Catlin (who was enthralled by the gorgeous colors, grace,

and inner strength of the native people), proposed that large sections of the plains be preserved "in their pristine beauty and wilderness, in a magnificent park, where the world could see, for ages to come, the native Indian in his classic attire, galloping his wild horses amid the fleeting herds of elk and buffalo."

This was not to be. However, in 1929, through the efforts of Senator Peter Norbeck, of South Dakota, Congress provided for the establishment of Badlands National Monument. After many homesteaders and ranchers, discouraged by the Dust Bowl days, had sold their land to the government, President Franklin D. Roosevelt officially proclaimed the monument in 1939. With the addition in 1976 of 133,300 acres formerly used as an Air Force gunnery range, the monument was more than doubled in size to its present 243,500 acres. Then in 1978 the area was officially redesig-

nated by Congress as a national park.

This raw, arid land seems to support little life. The temperature on summer days is in the 90s, sometimes over 100. Winter lasts half the year and blizzards go on for days. During June thundershowers tear away the soft surface of earth. Not too appealing, you might say. Nonetheless, here I can see the sweet-scented silver sagebrush and snowberry, fields of prickly pear and Spanish dagger, patches of cottonwood along the watercourse alive with birds, the coyote and badger reconnoitering around prairie dog towns, the bison, mule deer, and pronghorn (particularly near the wooded areas). Even in the bare cliff faces swifts and swallows build their nests, and often rock wrens do the same in the crevices, while an occasional eagle perches on a high butte. It's a land far from cities, and the name "Badland" is strictly a misnomer.

< RAIN POOL

Wind Cave
National Park

"BOXWORK" FORMATION ON CAVE CEILING

WIND CAVE WAS ESTABLISHED AS A NATIONAL PARK MORE BY ACCIDENT THAN DESIGN, but that doesn't take a thing away from it. As caves go, it has its special features, though they aren't what stand out in my mind. I think of it mainly as a natural tableau of the South Dakota plains in the period before the white man came, a one-of-a-kind reflecting the days of the Sioux, the buffalo, the antelope, and the prairie dog. Then too, Wind Cave is a lightly visited national park, which to my mind increases its charms.

As early as the 1890s the Wonderful Wind Cave Improvement Company opened passageways and built stairways for tourists in the unusual, thick limestone formation on the southeastern flank of the Black Hills. A few years later, however, the owners had a falling-out and a court battle. Largely because there seemed to be no solution, the area was turned over to the federal government. In this manner Wind Cave became the seventh national park, in 1903, the first cave so designated.

There were the natural features to commend it, of course. Geologists appear to have thought highly of it when they studied it in 1898. In the next few years reports of its beauty were published in national magazines. Though Wind Cave has nothing comparable to the huge rooms or flowstone formations of Carlsbad Caverns and Mammoth Cave, the delicately colored calcite, or crystalline, blades of "boxwork" constitute a rare formation found here and in few other places. Wind Cave, in fact, has more boxwork than any other known cave on earth.

At the mouth of the cave I can appreciate the source of its curious name. The strange action of the wind, often blowing in or out of the entrance, is caused by changes in air pressure. When pressure on the surface is high, as in fair weather, the wind blows inward; but when surface pressure falls, as before a storm, the air moves outward—dropping always from high to low.

Advancing into the rooms of the cave, I find displays of unusual "frostwork" and "popcorn" formations made by clusters of tiny white aragonite and calcite crystals, and colorful helictite bushes. Each of the rooms, or chambers, is different in size and appearance. The Fairgrounds is as large as an opera house or an amphitheater. The Post Office is adorned with boxwork clinging to the walls and ceiling like boxes in a post office. In the Garden of Eden, the boxwork is coated with white frost and the rocks are trimmed with little balls of popcorn. It's all something different from the stalagmites and stalactites in caves elsewhere.

Above ground, short grasses and medium-tall grasses, with a sprinkling of wild flowers, give a picture of the rich, rolling Great Plains. The park is relatively small, only a little over 28,000 acres, yet it suggests what the mid-continent must once have been like.

I rise early to observe the wildlife, remnants of millions of animals that once inhabited the land.

The sleek pronghorn antelope, singly and sometimes in pairs, roves across the hillsides. The swiftest of North America's large mammals, pronghorns are true natives found nowhere else in the world. Pronghorns have roamed the plains and deserts for at least the last million years in substantially the same form, a striking beauty against the open plains.

Small herds of huge, shaggy bison lumber slowly, though they can move with great speed, up to 35 miles per hour, and cover vast distances at a gallop. In 1800 there were about 40 million buffalo, but a century later there were fewer than 600 on the entire continent. I see bull elk feeding on grass, their massive antlers widespread. Once these magnificent animals were found in many parts of the continent, but uncontrolled killing reduced their numbers to remnant herds in isolated mountain areas.

Then there are prairie dogs, more like a squirrel than a dog, in one of the last of their significant "towns." Though hardly known today, at one time they numbered in the billions. As recently as the turn of this century, one dog town in Texas covered 25,000 square miles and contained 400 million animals. In the past 70 years, meeting humankind's material needs has caused obliteration of all but a few scattered colonies.

Fortunately, Wind Cave National Park protects one of these colonies. I watch with amusement the antics of the prairie dogs, particularly when a coyote or hawk sends them scurrying into burrows underground, and absorb lessons of interdependence. In the grand scheme of things on the plains, buffalo grazed the high grasses, enabling prairie dogs to watch for their enemies. The little dogs, in turn, grazed the short grasses, aiding the growth of plants favored by the pronghorn. The dogs also provided the food staple of the black-footed ferret, now the rarest mammal in North America—because the prairie dogs have dwindled so in number.

The vignette of the plains at Wind Cave provides an uplifting experience and memory. Here in 1912 a game preserve was established. The American Bison Society presented the first bison. Elk, pronghorn, and deer were added by others. Prairie dogs did not need to be introduced. The whole scene serves as a living link with early days that should never be forgotten. As long as the prairie dog and buffalo remain with us, so does our conscience.

OVERLEAF: EVERGLADES NATIONAL PARK >

"POPCORN" AND "FROSTWORK" IN THE GARDEN OF EDEN

THE EAST & THE MIDWEST

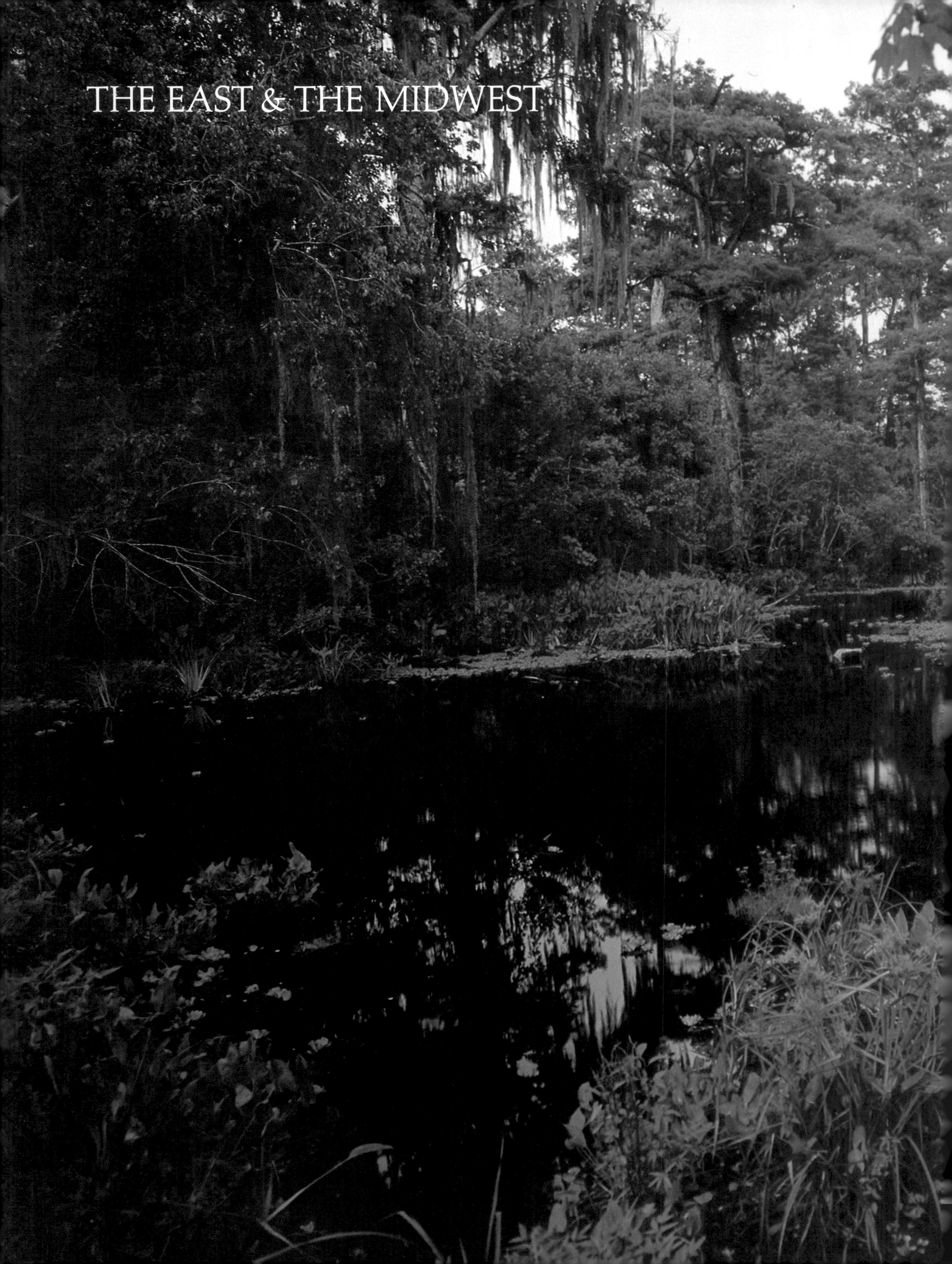

Voyageurs National Park

THE TIMBER FORTS AND OTHER PHYSICAL TRACES OF THE EARLY FRENCH-CANADIAN *VOYAGEURS* have long since vanished, but the land and waters they knew in their epic chapter of history are little altered. So I can visualize this network of lakes and streams in the heart of the North Woods as they saw it while transporting explorers, missionaries, and soldiers to the west and northwest, then returning to Montreal with their large birchbark canoes loaded with bales of fur.

Voyageurs, established in 1975 as the only national park in Minnesota, has all the wildness and immense scale associated with the northern shield region—a surface shaped by continental glaciation into some of the world's most tranquil scenery. Stands of fir, spruce, pine, aspen, and birch reach to the water's edge, broken here and there by bogs, cliffs, and sand beaches. Beavers thrive among the aspen. Throngs of native birds and numerous varieties of waterfowl feed in the bays, lagoons, and kettle holes. Wild rice grows in shallow bays and streams.

Large powerboats are permitted on the three big lakes—Namakan, Kabetogama, and Rainy, largest of all, covering 350 square miles. These lakes are too formidable for small boats

and canoes, but canoes are ideal to reach hidden bays and to explore small lakes away from the main arteries. With my companions, I travel alternately in both powerboat and canoe, one craft that telescopes distance, the other that brings fullness to time.

One day we stop at a rocky islet for a swim and lunch. That unusual bird of the wilderness, the loon, emerges on the surface; at least it shows its long, slender neck and ducklike head. It scans the scene, then descends for lower depths as suddenly as it had appeared. We swim in cool waters darkened by a high organic content, but as pure—well, almost as pure—as when the nomadic Chippewa roved the wilderness in small family groups searching for food.

The Chippewa (called Ojibwa on the Canadian side) were as much a part of the forest as trees, water, and wildlife. They believed that they were descended from forest animals, so their clan names and totemic emblems represented wildlife—the bear, loon, heron, moose, eagle, and catfish. The Indian traveled in a birchbark canoe, light and maneuverable, which he paddled while kneeling, without benefit of centerboard or seats. In winter, when lakes and rivers froze, he set aside the canoe and brought out snowshoes, toboggan,

and sled, all of which he made himself. He managed without a snowmobile.

On our rocky islet long-stemmed wintergreen plants wait to provide their red berries as food for birds. Just beyond our touch a brazen Canada jay, the notorious "camp robber," signals that it has no intention of waiting. A hermit thrush sings a flutelike song while scurrying over the ground in search of insects. Our little refuge is bordered by a forest of tall, tapering spruce and balsam fir. Here we try to capture for a brief instant that sense of harmony with nature the Indian knew instinctively throughout his life.

Kettle Falls Hotel, at the extreme east end of Rainy Lake, is a link to a more recent era of trapper, trader, fisherman, and lumberjack. This well-preserved, odd little backwoods hotel seems to be in place here. Nature has played a queer trick on the mapmakers, for at Kettle Falls I stand on Minnesota soil and look south into Canada.

Farther east I arrive at Crane Lake Gorge, one of Voyageurs' scenic spectaculars, where the Vermillion River tumbles through a narrow chasm between vertical rock walls before flowing into the lake. The whole park is filled with such fresh and sparkling vistas, making it a living storehouse of beauty.

METAMORPHIC ROCK ALONG KABETOGAMA LAKE

Isle Royale National Park

ONE OF THE NICEST PARTS ABOUT BEING ON ISLE ROYALE IS THAT I DON'T HAVE TO LISten to the noise of automobiles. Motor transportation in a boat or seaplane may be necessary to reach it and there are motors of one kind or another on the island, but at least no motorcars. And no roads.

The main island of this rocky fortress in Lake Superior (closer to Canada than to the nearest point in Upper Michigan) is 45 miles long and nine miles across at its widest point. Surrounding it are some 200 small islands and clusters of rocky islets.

While walking along the shore near fjord-like Rock Harbor I meet a young couple traveling in a canoe laden with ten days' rations. They pitch their tent on rock clearings overlooking small offshore islands and then go exploring. They can also follow streams to connect with inland lakes—a marvelous way to travel on Isle Royale, where the deep bays and the islands provide miles of protected waterways.

Colored pebbles, even semiprecious greenstones, adorn the wave-swept shores. Old lava flows formed the early rocks of Isle Royale. During the glacial period the island was buried beneath a mile-thick sheet of ice; its level receded in several stages, each stage marked by formation of a new shoreline. The smoothly rounded gravel and cobbles indicate an earlier beachline. The soil on the island's stony foundation is still only a few inches to a few feet in depth. There are no monarchs among the trees, though Isle Royale is a wonderful meeting ground of hardwoods and conifers.

Following trails through forests and along rocky shores, bogs and swamps, and open meadows, I observe hundreds of species of wild flowers, including some—such as yellow lady's-slipper, swamp candle loosestrife, bog kalmia, purple-fringed orchid, and fringed polygala—that are distinctive, due to isolation from mainland influences. This isolation, in fact, makes Isle Royale an ideal field laboratory for studying the natural sciences, as all national parks should be. Various research

BIRCHES

SUNSET AT HUGINNIN COVE

SPRING GREENERY

projects here cover ferns and flowering plants, vegetational succession, fish, and the moose-wolf relationship.

These studies would never have been possible without the park. Concern over the growing number of summer homes and hotels on Isle Royale when excursion boats increased its accessibility led to pleas for its protection. Authorized in 1931, the national park was established nine years later.

The story of the Isle Royale wolf and moose is a dramatic national park saga. At the turn of the century there were no moose on Isle Royale. Exactly when they arrived is not known, though it may have been in 1912, when the lake froze. This largest member of the deer family found browse on the island and flourished. The population exploded. Adolph Murie visited Isle Royale in 1929 and 1930 and reported signs of moose overwhelming their food supply, ravaging and stripping everything. By the mid-thirties there were almost 3,000 moose; mass starvation set in, and soon their numbers declined to 500. A fire in 1936 destroyed one-fourth of the island's timber, clearing the way for new growth. The

moose population rose to 800, followed by another die-off. Such fluctuations are likely in a long-term cycle, particularly in the absence of a creature's natural foe.

Then, in the winter of 1948–49, timber wolves crossed the 15-mile stretch of ice and began to prey on the moose. Research biologists, attracted to study the relationship between these two species, have observed that the wolves claim the old, the diseased, the heavily parasitized, and the weak young among the moose. As a result of natural predation, the moose herd is considered one of the healthiest on the continent, with a relatively stable population. The moose-wolf studies at Isle Royale are now widely cited among wildlife professionals to emphasize the values of predation.

While hiking along the shore of Lake Ojibway, I hear a raven call, then moments later watch a pair fly by on a steady course. I catch sight of a moose shuffling down to the lake, huge and seemingly ungainly, wading in without pausing to feed on the succulent pond weeds. My imagination suggests that there may be a wolf nearby, but none appears.

Acadia National Park

AS NATIONAL PARKS GO, ACADIA IS DEFINITELY SMALL IN SIZE. YELLOWSTONE COVERS MORE than 2 million acres, Acadia less than 38,000. Acadia has never been ranked among the superspectacular parks either. I recall the gentleman who headed the National Park Service for almost ten years and never once visited Acadia, which indicates where it rates among those in charge.

That director never knew what he missed, while he had the chance. In my book Acadia is a treasure in a thousand and one ways. It embraces the finest surviving fragment of the New England shoreline, virtually all that's left of the rockbound Maine coast we Americans learn about from the poems we study in grade school. I only wish there were more of it.

The first national park in the East, Acadia is the only one in New England. It was established in 1919 as Lafayette National Park and renamed in 1929. Most of the park is on Mount Desert Island, with smaller sections on the tip of Schoodic Peninsula to the east across Frenchman Bay and on Isle au Haut—a wilderness reached only by boat—to the southwest, plus a few scattered islands.

I love to be at the windswept 1,530-foot crest of Cadillac Mountain, high above the sea. Brilliant vistas free of cities unfold in all directions, extending to the granite outline of Mount Katahdin far to the north, the highest point in Maine. Below, down through woodlands and past shimmering lakes and the villages rimming coves and harbors, Mount Desert Island falls to the sea. To the east and the south, the shining ocean, sprinkled with islands, stretches to the horizon.

Here I get the feel of history—of a nation born of the sea and bred on salt spray. Very likely the early explorers who sailed along this stretch of the North American coast relied on the distinctive outline of Mount Desert Island as a navigation aid. Champlain landed here in 1604 during his exploration of French Acadia; then the British steered their way past the landmark to New England ports. In time schooners and brigs were built in every cove, and offshore fishing fleets whitened the horizon with hundreds of sails.

The forces of nature are manifest everywhere. The slopes that looked bare and raw following the disastrous fire of 1947 are now covered with sun-loving shrubs and a growing forest of birch, aspen, oak, and maple; in time the slower-growing spruce and fir will again claim the forest. In the interior the landscape of deep-blue lakes shielded by steep slopes tells the story of ancient glacial action—of massive waves of ice piling rock debris in some

places, gouging lakes in others, and shaving peaks. Today this land remains under snow each year until April, when the delicate trailing arbutus signals the beginning of spring with its pinkish-white flowers; it is first in a procession of many species of flowering plants, including 20 kinds of orchids, Labrador tea, and azalea. I like to follow the low wetlands to search for signs of nesting ducks and beaver dams and for the sight of a great blue heron poking its bill underwater for tadpoles, insects, or snakes.

Down at the shore, I watch waves at work in the endless battle of the sea to wear down the granite. At Anemone Cave pounding waters have tunneled 85 feet into the hard rock. I am fascinated by the profusion of growing things amidst the tidal turmoil—rockweed hanging from the wall, algae encrusting the

floor, kelp swaying in the waves, flowerlike anemone, and that brightly-colored sea snail, the dog whelk. In the struggle to survive, each feeds on the other, and all compete for nutrients. The shrimplike barnacle solves one of its problems by sealing its shell so that even while clinging securely to naked rock, it can remain dry 95 percent of the time.

With friends I cruise through Frenchman Bay into the ocean, looking up at Great Head, the highest headland of the Atlantic coast, Hunters Head, and Bass Harbor Head, all on Acadia's rocky brim. I enjoy a clear view of the cliffs and hidden coves. Cormorants and gulls congregate on a rocky shoal, reminding me how vital islets and islands are as nesting grounds of seabirds. Luckily, a few islands are included in the park. Very probably there should be more.

AZALEA AT FOOT OF CADILLAC MOUNTAIN

EAGLE LAKE

Shenandoah National Park

SHENANDOAH IS THE NATIONAL PARK NEAREST TO MY HOME. COME TO THINK OF IT, IT MUST be closer to more people than any other national park. Years ago the parks were strictly a "Western" heritage. Then new ones were established in the East, with special impetus during the administrations of Presidents Herbert Hoover and Franklin D. Roosevelt, both of whom were personally interested in a truly *national* park system.

In the case of Shenandoah, the park came not too late, but with too little. It extends along the crest of the Blue Ridge Mountains in Virginia for a distance of 105 miles. But the park is never very wide. While on the crest I view the ridges and slopes extending east and west and wish that more of them could have been included. That might once have been, when this was still remote backcountry and land values were low; it would be difficult, though not impossible, to accomplish now.

Not that I don't love the park or appreciate all the effort that went into setting it aside. It's pure delight to go there in any season, to be somewhere among the 60 mountain peaks ranging from 2,000 to 4,000 feet that reach up to blend their summits with billows of bluish haze—to look out across the Piedmont Plateau to the east and over the Shenandoah Valley and the main ranges of the Appalachians to the west. Despite the narrow dimensions and the main-stem parkway called the Skyline Drive running down the middle, despite the fact that the mountains were lived in and logged over, there are still sequestered corners—pockets of primeval hemlock, ancient oaks that escaped the axe, and lively second-growth forests sheltering flowering shrubs, vines, and herbs, all parts of the rich Southern Appalachian flora.

Shenandoah National Park was first approved by Congress in 1926 (when Acadia was the only national park east of the Mississippi), but complete acceptance depended on the people of Virginia acquiring the land and deeding it to the government. It took almost ten years to raise $1¼ million from private contributions and another $1 million through appropriation by the Virginia legislature. The "father of the park" was George Freeman Pollock, naturalist, conservationist, and owner of the Skyland resort, known for his uncanny way with snakes as well as with people of all classes. His principal ally, Harry F. Byrd, Governor of the Commonwealth and later U.S. Senator, climbed Old Rag Mountain at least once every year until he could no longer walk—and he knew every other peak in the park almost as well.

BEARFENCE MOUNTAIN

The mountains were lived in by the backwoods farmers of yesteryear, mostly Scotch-Irish, Germans, Huguenots, and English. Their grandparents and parents had settled in the valleys and coves, with fertile bottomland and meadows, but succeeding generations moved into subvalleys, along creek branches, and up the steep hillsides to scrabble for a hard living. In the neighborhood of Skyland not a mountaineer had been to school and only a few could sign their names. Most of them were glad to sell their land to the state and get out, but some resisted, clinging to their homes.

Even a president's personal landholding— Herbert Hoover's fishing camp on the Rapidan River—became part of the new park. Soon after taking office he had assigned an aide to find a summer retreat on a trout stream within 100 miles of Washington, at an elevation of 2,500 feet or more. "Fishing is a constant reminder of the democracy of life, of humility and of human frailty—for all men are equal before fishes," said the president, who was himself a rather modest and unassuming person by nature.

On the trail to Whiteoak Canyon, which Pollock called the most beautiful ravine in the whole park and perhaps in the eastern United States, I pass a lovely patch of giant virgin hemlock, known as the Limberlost, to enter a wild and water-splashed garden of rock, vines, and shrubs. The rocks of the Blue Ridge are very old and have been rounded by wind, water, and frost. Shafts of sunlight illuminate the brownish-red trunks of the hemlocks. The sun filters through the leaves of hardwoods to dance across the waters of Whiteoak Falls. Resting below the falls, I hear the chorus of green frogs. Quite by accident my foot overturns a rock to disturb a red-backed salamander. Sometimes I think there must be a salamander under every rock in the Appalachian wild forest. Many species of salamanders are native to these mountains, found on the rocky, mossy floors of their own stream valleys and nowhere else.

Another day I climb precipitous "Old Raggedy," or Old Rag, an unmistakable granite landmark east of the main range and the most celebrated peak in the park. To reach the top I follow the Ridge Trail from the town of Nethers at the east side of the base. It's a challenging all-day climb, a 7.7-mile circuit hike skirting huge boulders and even through a cave. Once on top—the crest is almost five miles long—I wind around jumbled boulders which tell of an earlier age when these massive

rocks were torn loose from the mountain. Like Senator Byrd, I could sit on the summit for hours watching with intense pleasure the shadows, the changing colors, and the majesty and grandeur of the Blue Ridge.

Forests are the essence of the Blue Ridge. Walking through the woods, I encounter many species of trees and try to identify them by the shape of their leaves—the wavy edges of chestnut oak, the pointed lobes of red oak, the square tips of the yellow poplar, and the small oval forms of the black locust. Normally the locust appears spindly and insignificant; foresters tend to regard it as a "weed tree." In Shenandoah it's one of the first trees that take hold in old meadows and fields, in time providing shade for young oaks, the bigger trees that follow. In April or May, however, locusts have their own brief moment of glory, displaying clusters of white, cream-colored, and pink flowers, lovely and fragrant, drawing droves of bees.

Here and there in the mixed forest a stunted chestnut rises out of the roots of an old stump. The chestnut was possibly the most loved and useful tree in America. It grew into

TRILLIUMS IN DECIDUOUS FOREST

a towering giant, found almost everywhere in the eastern forest. Its straight-grained and durable lumber was suited for many uses. Its nuts were a delicacy to squirrels, bears, and wild turkeys. Then the mysterious chestnut blight, caused by a tiny fungus introduced from Asia around 1900, struck havoc. In the southern mountains the chestnut was almost totally eliminated by the early thirties. Generally the chestnut exists now only as gray, dead, twisted stumps and logs and as sprouts growing from surviving roots. I've watched the sprouts; they live for a few years before they in turn are struck down by the disease. Recently, however, they seem to be more vigorous, lasting longer and producing more flowers in late June and early July. Maybe it's my imagination or just wishful thinking, but then again, maybe the chestnut really is on its way back.

In late March the higher elevations of the park are still cool, though spring flowers and budding trees begin their show, with hepatica, red maple, and bloodroot among the early arrivals. I walk across one of the gaps and see trillium, columbine, and spring beauty. So many living elements of the forest environment are overlooked because they are small. In spring small and humble plants demand to be recognized. I do not know them by name, but their form and color remind me that a wild forest is composed of many parts, and the more complex and diverse the community, the healthier and more productive the forest.

Then follows the green season of early summer, when plants are making food from sunlight and the whole pyramid of life seems at its most productive. The mountain wilderness finds voice in the songs of rushing streams and in birds raising their young. It's the time when spotted fawns and bear cubs first scout the earth's dominion that will be theirs.

Every season in the mountains holds some special treat. Many visitors return to the Skyline Drive each autumn when the slopes are a blaze of color extending to the horizon from both sides of the crest. Winter is the least known season. On cold, crisp days evergreens stand out boldly against the snowy white background and icicles cascade over the rocky cliffs. The meadows are covered by a foot or two of snow; a strong wind whips the leafless slopes. Many animals are hibernating but life goes on, as I can tell by the sight of squirrels and an occasional bird, of deer reduced to chewing on twigs, of the tracks and droppings of bears in the snow. On a winter night the stars seem to be brighter than ever, and I feel glad to know this time of year in this mountain park.

Great Smoky Mountains National Park

IT IS RAINING IN THE SMOKIES. WHENEVER I COME INTO THESE MOUNTAINS IT SEEMS TO BE RAINing, but I have learned never to complain about the Smokies' weather. The rain is soft and warm, a summer spray, the kind of friendly rain that reminds me the earth is good. It splashes the air with smells of new life in the woods.

I have been hiking with friends, climbing uphill. Soon after the rain relents we stop to spread our lunch on a rocky island, surrounded by rolling haze and, at our fingertips, by summer-blooming herbs, mosses, and dwarfed rosy-pink Carolina rhododendron, the "deer laurel" that grows in the southern mountains and nowhere else.

A towhee flicks her long, rounded tail while flitting upward toward the spruce and fir, near which she builds her summer nest. An ensemble of tiny winter wrens, normally reserved, proclaim their presence with melodious high-pitched trilling and favor us with their rare antiphonal song. As soon as one utters the last bubbling *crrrip*, another begins for round after tuneful round. In this setting "the Great Smoky Mountains" seems to be another name for paradise.

Rains leave the air almost constantly moist, the ground damp. As the southern sun warms the ground a light fog ascends the slope, a bluish or smokelike mist rolling over the gaps and hovering just below the summits. Nourished by rain and rushing streams, plant life is luxuriant and varied. "There is not a cranny in the rocks of the Great Smokies, not a foot of the wild glen, but harbors something lovable and rare," wrote Horace Kephart, outdoorsman and author who lived in and loved these mountains.

Kephart is best remembered for his classic book, *Camping and Woodcraft*. He also wrote *Our Southern Highlanders*, about the people of the Smokies in the days before it was a national park. "It is not the clearing but the unfenced wilderness that is the camper's real home," Kephart wrote. "He is brother to that good old friend of mine who in gentle satire of our formal gardens and close-cropped lawns was wont to say, 'I love the unimproved works of God.'"

I am a Kephart fan. I know the family he lived with and the site of his grave in Bryson City, North Carolina, the story of his death in an automobile accident, and a great deal more. One day I hike to his favorite campsite at the Bryson Place, deep in the woods between Thomas Divide and Noland Divide. On the way up the trail a timber rattler slithers out of the brush and my companion kills it with a

RAINBOW FALLS

ROARING FORK CREEK

stick (while I realize his action is instinctive, I wonder why it needs to be). The rattles continue to vibrate after the snake is dead. We find the Bryson Place overgrown with blackberry bushes, holly, dogwood, sassafras, grapevine, and sumac. An owl, sensing disturbance, flies out of the jungle growth to head across tangled leucothoe, or dog hobble, and through a grove of white pine and hemlock.

Everywhere around me are the unimproved works of God. Before the park was established, in 1930, there were little backcountry settlements and logging camps and logging railroads and herds of cattle grazing on the grassy mountaintops. Hiking the trails, I find vestiges of settlement days—rocky foundations of old houses, vine-shrouded bricks, patches of daffodils and daisies in bloom, gaunt and ghostly fruit trees that refuse to die, and graveyards still maintained with paper flowers at the headstones to brighten shadowy woodlands. But for the most part the mountains have reverted to their own, progressing through the natural cycle, and today the cornfield of three decades ago is a young forest of infinite variety, taking its place alongside older, more primitive portions of the park that were never cultivated and where trees were never cut.

Plants, flowers, and trees are to the Smokies what granite domes are to Yosemite and geysers to Yellowstone. Professor Asa Gray, the noted Harvard botanist, once said that he encountered more species of trees within the 30 miles west of Asheville, North Carolina, than could be observed elsewhere from the Atlantic coast to the Rocky Mountains or in traveling from England clear across Europe to Turkey. And he hadn't yet reached the stronghold of the Great Smokies.

Great Smoky Mountains National Park covers more than half a million acres, embracing some of the oldest mountains on earth. Their foundations were laid on the floor of a shallow sea over 500 million years ago, and their loftiness was produced about 200 million years ago during a long period of earth upheavals called the Appalachian Revolution. The mountains now rise like a citadel of peaks astride the North Carolina-Tennessee border for a distance of 70 miles—the masterwork of the Appalachian chain, the highest mountain mass in eastern America.

The park's acreage is divided almost equally between the two states. Looking upward from the Tennessee side, I see Mount Le Conte towering over the landscape (though at 6,593 feet it's about 50 feet lower than Clingmans Dome, the tallest peak in the park). Once atop Le Conte I can see all the peaks rolling to the horizon like green waves. At sunset I walk to Cliff Top to view hundreds of square miles of mountains, lowlands, and East Tennessee towns, the lights of Knoxville ahead, and the western horizon darkening until night color prevails.

The Smokies escaped the icy tongue of glaciers and gave sanctuary to many plant species fleeing the frigid North. As a result, today it is the meeting ground of northern and southern types of forests. Flowers and shrubs are everywhere—in the densest woods, in the open clearings, and on the treeless, tangled heath balds of the higher mountaintops. There are 50 different kinds of lily, 22 kinds of violet. In early spring, after the thawing of winter's chill, the pent-up forest comes rapidly into bloom, usually with a burst of spring beauty and hepatica. Then dogwood arrives to brighten the barren woods, spreading its blossoms—chalky white or as pink as a cloud. In the deep shade of the gaps the moist ground beneath the dogwood turns white too with snow trillium, the pale flower of the trinity, bearing three green leaflets, three green sepals,

and three white petals. The dwarf mountain iris glows in purple flower among sword-shaped leaves. The red and yellow columbine, with buttercup leaves, sways in a soft breeze, awaiting the ruby-throated hummingbird.

Then the kalmia, or mountain laurel, which local people called "ivy," tufts the ridges with white and rose. Thickets of pink azalea, which mountaineers called "wild honeysuckle" (its blossoms do resemble those of the honeysuckle vine), spread over the hillsides, soon to be joined by the blazing flame azalea, which the pioneer colonial naturalist William Bartram described as "the most gay and brilliant flowering shrub yet known." At Gregory Bald in late June wild azaleas range from pure white through all the pinks, yellows, and flames to deep saturated red. June is the month of rhododendron too. It begins with purple rhododendron on the mountain slopes, followed by the densely flowered piedmont, or punctatum, growing waist high; and the towering catawba, or rose-pink, blooming at different altitudes into July and the rest of the summer; and the *Rhododendron maximum*,

forming a giant garden of waxy-white to deep pink under streamside hemlocks.

Rainbow Falls, Laurel Falls, and the scores of other cascades are banked with flowering shrubs. One day I head upward from the Greenbrier, deep into virgin woods to Ramsay Cascade, because I have heard it called the most beautiful falls in the park. The trail passes towering hemlock, 400-year-old tulip poplars, black cherry, and white ash, along streams thickly shaded with rhododendron. The tulip poplar is my favorite tree of the southern hardwood forest. Sometimes in the sheltered coves it grows more than 190 feet high with a diameter of eight to ten feet. It's really a magnolia and produces a large tulip-like flower.

Along the trail the Ramsay Prong of the Middle Prong of the Little Pigeon River running down from Mount Guyot has a great roar in its throat that drowns out conversation. This is not an easy climb; it cannot be made hurriedly. My reward, however, is to sit at the edge of Ramsay Cascade and feel the cool air current and the spray of water splashing and shouting while it tumbles 100 feet into a shallow-pan pool before proceeding on its way.

AZALEA AT NEWFOUND GAP

At Newfound Gap on the historic Appalachian Trail, which runs along the crest of the Smokies, I can touch the mist and watch it rise to ring the peaks in wreaths of haze. It was here at the crescent-shaped masonry platform and wall, straddling the boundary line between Tennessee and North Carolina, that President Franklin D. Roosevelt dedicated the park on Labor Day, 1940. On that day the nation deeded the Smokies back—back to their own destiny. Following the ceremony it took 10,000 automobiles until dark to disperse. The land for the park had been bought and paid for and presented to the government by the people of the two states in which it lies, and by $5,000,000 in matching funds donated by John D. Rockefeller, Jr., as a living memorial to his mother. It was one of numerous bequests he made to the national parks' cause.

West of Newfound Gap, I tramp past the rocky ribs of Clingmans Dome to Silers Bald, thick with wild grass, near the point where the spruce forest reaches the southern limit of its range. Once I came this way with Harvey Broome, who, for more than 50 years until he died, hiked and camped all over the Smokies, in all seasons. We shared summer rains, and he knew the winter frosts as well. The government planned to punch a new road across the mountains through Silers Bald, but Harvey led a public effort that blocked it. The mountains, of course, look much better as they are,

FOG-SHROUDED NEWFOUND GAP

GRANITE LAYERS OF CLINGMANS DOME

Mammoth Cave National Park

AT MAMMOTH CAVE I REALIZE THAT I AM WALKING THROUGH ONE OF THE GREAT NATURAL wonders of the world, that the processes I can see at work below ground are as marvelous as those above the surface, that formations in caves hold as much appeal and value as the formations in the high peaks of the Rockies or in the spectacular color country of the Southwest.

Mammoth is America's most historic cave. It has drawn visitors to south-central Kentucky since its discovery in 1798. Tourists came first by stagecoach, then by steamer up the Green River. They entered with headlamps, had a sense of adventure, and called it "the greatest cave that ever was." The Emperor of Brazil came to see it for himself, and so did the Grand Duke of Russia. About one-half mile from the Historic Entrance I walk through the underground chasm now called Booth's Amphitheater, where Edwin Booth recited Hamlet's soliloquy, and then through Ole Bull's Concert Hall, where the Norwegian violinist performed. Jenny Lind, the Swedish nightingale, performed here too, shattering the subterranean stillness with her golden voice.

In time, however, the cave outgrew its role as a showplace for entertainment and was recognized for higher values worth preserving in a national park. Though authorized in 1926, the park wasn't fully established until 1941.

Nobody knows how mammoth Mammoth Cave really is. Up to now some 150 miles of the cave, extending down to five levels, the lowest 360 feet below the surface, have been mapped. With miles of passages and subterranean levels still unexplored, it may be the largest cave system in the world. Geologists call the area where the park is located the Southern Sinkhole Plain, but local people are apt to refer to it as the "Land of 10,000 Sinks." The sinkholes and the formation of Mammoth Cave have been intimately related over millions of years, for a longer time than I can imagine. The same forces continue to form new passages and to decorate old ones, thus enhancing the visual beauty of this underground wilderness.

Stalactites, stalagmites, lily pads and other flower shapes, columns, and draping formations are everywhere. So are unusual domes and pits, with great vertical height and grooves, or "fluting," formed by the solvent effect of trickling water. Almost every formation of any size has a name. The largest in the park, a massive flowstone deposit 75 feet high and almost 50 feet wide—fluted stalactites spilling from a lofty ledge—is called Frozen Niagara, which seems quite right. Mammoth Dome is almost as high as a 20-story building. There are others called Bottomless Pit, Great Wall of China, Rainbow Dome, Theater Curtain, Macaroni Factory, Fat Man's Misery, and the beautiful Snowball Room, where lunch is served. But what's in a name? I can look at any of these for a few minutes from one angle or another and let my imagination choose some altogether different name for them, or maybe none at all.

The gypsum formations are restricted to the drier portions, where slow leaching of calcium sulfate through porous limestone forces the crystals outward. Then they grow and often curve, much like ice crystals from a wet soil during winter, crusting an entire wall or ceiling with fanciful forms. They seem to take the shape of flowers, pendants, and gargoyles. The Mammoth Gypsum Wall is a riot of what appear to be spiders, needles, fluffy masses like cotton candy, and flowers—all composed of fragile gypsum crystals.

There are living creatures in this wonderland that cannot see it. At Crystal Lake, a part of Echo River five levels below the surface, I observe blind minnow-sized fish. They have no use for their eyes, and darkness has robbed them of their pigment. I learn that there are blind, or eyeless, crayfish as well. They remind me of the famous flightless cormorants of the Galápagos Islands, which have demiwings but cannot fly—nor do they need to, because their food is plentiful and they have no enemies.

Although human intervention has altered much of the earth's surface, the marvels underground have developed and evolved undisturbed over the millennia. It is unfortunate that they should be so easily disruptable. A single brush of the hand destroys crystalline formations a hundred thousand years in the making. Continued exposure to artificial light stimulates the growth of algae that, in turn, change the coloring and texture of formations.

The formations themselves are dependent on a certain amount of moisture seeping down from the surface. So the Green River, winding 25 miles across scenic hills and valleys on the surface of the park, is the key to active circulation of underground and surface waters, assuring that further passages will continue to be formed at the lower levels for a new world of hidden beauty.

FORMATIONS ALONG BRIDGEWAY

Hot Springs National Park

IN A SENSE HOT SPRINGS MAY BE CALLED THE FIRST NATIONAL PARK, CONSIDERING THAT IT'S THE OLDEST reservation set aside by Congress for the perpetual use and enjoyment of the people. This was in 1832, long before anybody was thinking of preserving Yellowstone or Yosemite. It wasn't called a national park—that came much later, in 1921—but the idea was there.

Hot Springs lacks the size or space that one usually associates with the national park concept; it covers less than 5,900 acres. Besides, the heart of the park is in the midst of a bustling resort city, but I like it anyway (and I've never even taken one of the mineral baths).

Being in Hot Springs brings to my mind the history of baths, which have been part of human culture since the time of the Greeks and Romans and probably earlier. Almost everywhere that heated, pungent springs are found, so too are baths. In earlier times the idea reached beyond mere cleanliness into cultism and religion, which conjures a whole set of themes to explore. American Indians

believed in the therapy of hot springs and doubtless knew this section of the Ouachita Mountains in what is now Arkansas. I have read in some reports that battles may have been fought to control the land, and in others that Indians came together in peace to bathe in the sacred, healing waters. Maybe they did both, depending on the tribes and the period in history.

Hernando de Soto is thought to have sampled the springs in 1541. If only we could see them as he did, say in the same natural condition as the thermal features in Yellowstone, that would really make for a superb national park. Still, the waters flow as hot now as then and for reasons never clearly determined. The springs are along a fault, an ancient break in the earth's crust, on the west slope of Hot Springs Mountain. Geologists theorize that when rainwater sinks into the earth it rises along tilted layers of rock to emerge through the fault and may be heated by molten rocks or radioactive minerals deep in the earth's interior, by friction, or by chemical reactions underground.

In any event, the mineral water is collected from 45 springs into a huge reservoir for use in commercial bathhouses operating on federal land under national park regulations. These baths are designed to relieve the sick and help the fit stay in condition. They must accomplish something, because people keep coming. Two other springs still emerge naturally, with a most unusual phenomenon present—a rare species of blue-green algae thriving in the hot pools. Algae are normally found in cool ponds, lakes, and streams, and this particular species has been found at only one other place on this continent, Banff in the Canadian Rockies.

I like this little national park because beyond the city of Hot Springs it preserves an undisturbed Ouachita woodland, varying in elevation from 600 feet on the valley floor to 1,200 feet on the summits of rocky hills. Along its 18-mile network of hiking trails I find evidences of varied species of wildlife, of birds, lizards, salamanders, and small mammals. Wild flowers bloom in the oak, hickory, and pine forests, providing a pleasant surprise for those who venture outside the city.

TOP OF HOT SPRINGS MOUNTAIN

Everglades National Park

AT THE SOUTHWESTERN TIP OF FLORIDA, THE EVERGLADES STILL COVER AN AREA LARGER than the state of Delaware, even though great portions have been diked, drained, and developed over the past 30 years. I remember the Everglades of years gone by, when they seemed to go on forever and when there were panthers almost in Miami's backyard. The final vestige, a wilderness of a kind found nowhere else, is entirely in the national park, which was established in 1947. Some of the birds, reptiles, and mammals of the Everglades are either rare or, like the habitats that support them, are found here alone. I could observe them for days or weeks on end without losing interest, except, I fear, in summer—a season all its own, dominated by aggressive and ferocious mosquitoes to which I prefer to cede the field.

Here the Caribbean tropics meet the temperate zone in an aquatic setting, for the Everglades are half-land, half-water. A nearly flat river—the "river of grass"—has flowed since time immemorial without disturbance (until our time) from Lake Okeechobee in central Florida south for 100 miles to merge with the waters of Florida Bay and the Gulf of Mexico. The low islands, or keys, in the bay have always seemed to me more like the Bahamas than like anything on the mainland. Clusters of trees and dense vegetation in the open glades form "islands" of land called "hammocks." The hardwood trees, more typical of the West Indies than of Florida, include the mahogany, the strangler fig, and the coppery-barked gumbo-limbo. In other sections, bald cypress and pine forests of the southern swamps prevail. The lush vegetation includes giant ferns, colorful air plants growing on tree barks, and some 80 species of orchids. Then there are the tangled mangroves and the saw-grass prairie, flat but never dull.

The mangrove forests I find intriguing, perhaps because they are so unlike forests on dry land or possibly because they are vanishing in other parts of the world, banished to oblivion by human inroads. One day in the Everglades, while canoeing with a young park ranger on the Hells Bay Trail, I feel utterly surrounded and encompassed by mangroves as we tunnel through tangled thickets of these unusual trees rising on stilted arching roots to form a canopy 50 to 75 feet high. The trail is marked with white floats, but we contrive somehow to lose our way repeatedly, much to the ranger's embarrassment. The mangrove forest is full of mysterious beauty; waters darkened by tannic acid mirror the jungle in striking clarity. A yellow-crowned heron soars over the trees and breaks the quiet with a shrill squawk. I observe egrets and ibises on the mudflats, the dark back of a limpkin barely visible as the bird digs for snails among the mangrove roots, a brown pelican in the top of a small tree, a blue-winged teal scooping food from the shallows.

The mangroves, tolerating salt water and thus growing where most plants would be lost, are vibrant with life. The nutrient-rich brackish mixture of salt and fresh waters sustains crustaceans, mollusks, and insects, and they in turn serve the nursery of shrimp and fish of the deep sea, such as tarpon, pompano, and mackerel. Another day we follow the 100-mile Wilderness Waterway. Traveling in the powered patrol boat from the town of Everglades, at the northwest end of the park, we weave along the coast of the Gulf of Mexico among the shallow Ten Thousand Islands, which Rachel Carson called one of the great mangrove swamps of the world. Overhead I see a wood ibis, or "flinthead," whose tribe represents the only stork in the United States —a huge bird with pure white feathers con-trasting with jet-black wingtips. Then I spot a bald eagle, perched in a high nest, and the ranger explains that the park has a population of between 150 and 200, now believed stable and hatching an average of 40 per year. That's good news! Offshore is a school of frolicking porpoises, then pelicans gliding along the palm-fringed shoreline, and great white herons spreading their immense wings; I catch glimpses of wondrous species, but all too fast. Carson described the Ten Thousand Islands as "a wilderness untamed and almost unvisited by man." It takes seven days to cover the Wilderness Waterway by canoe and only one by powerboat, but traveling by machine makes man a part of the machinery, rather than a part of nature.

Over the centuries the rhythms of life have wrought wonders in the Everglades. In summer, rains from swelling clouds normally flood this area. Wildlife disperses into the glades and swamps. Then, during the dry months of late winter and spring, surface waters evaporate and the glades dry up. Wild creatures congregate at the ponds that remain. I watch

HYACINTH- AND CYPRESS-LINED CANAL

an alligator at work, rearranging things, rooting out dense stands of saw grass in the shallow bog, making "gator holes" that give it room to maneuver. These patches of open water serve other animals' interests as well as the gator's. During drought the gator holes, filled with water, attract fish, turtles, and many frogs and lizards; water birds come to feed on crawfish, snails, and lizards.

In its original condition, southern Florida displayed one of the greatest wildlife spectacles on earth. There is still incredible variety, from crustaceans and shellfish, snakes, deer, raccoons, and possums up to panthers and black bears. Lagoons provide pasture for the manatee, Florida's strange air-breathing "sea cow," and the swamps serve as habitat for the blunt-nosed alligator, which sticks to fresh water, and the rare, vanishing long-snouted crocodile, which prefers its water salty. Among America's rarest and loveliest water birds, the roseate spoonbill feeds in quiet brackish mangrove pools.

Today the wildlife populations are only a memory of the throngs found here 30 years ago. Through a web of dikes and drainage canals, the once-natural flow of fresh water is now controlled by man. The summer-wet, winter-dry water cycle has been disrupted and the water table lowered, allowing salt water to intrude inland, and all life systems have been damaged. The partially completed jetport at the edge of the park poses another threat. The wilderness is reduced to a fragile copy of its former self.

I somehow feel sure, however, that what does remain of the Everglades will always be there, for how much poorer America would be without it.

SAW GRASS AND PALMS

Virgin Islands National Park

ALKING ALONG THE BEACHES, I AM STRUCK BY THE DRAMATIC CONTRAST BETWEEN the white sands underfoot, the deep blue of the Caribbean offshore, and the tropical green of the flora covering most of the island of St. John rising behind and above me. Where, I wonder, did this Elysian fragment come from?

St. John is one of the U.S. Virgin Islands, in the Caribbean east of Puerto Rico. When volcanoes erupted deep in the ocean, the buckling crust raised rock islands above the surface of the sea. Since then the beaches of St. John have been a zone of arriving life; the current and tides deliver some species of plants and animals, insects, eggs, seeds, and seedlings, with other species riding the winds to form new colonies here. The sands, however, are derived from coral, created over long periods of time by living beings—many, many thousand beings—with bodies formed of protoplasm (as our own bodies are formed).

Snorkeling is to the Virgin Islands what hiking is to the Smokies. At Trunk Bay Beach, one of St. John's loveliest, is the world's first underwater trail, replete with labels on glass plates attached to submerged formations along the way. But the coral reefs are so fascinating to me that snorkeling is not enough, and I learn to scuba dive, not proficiently but adequately. I never dive alone, but now I go deeper than with snorkel and stay longer. Most of the offshore waters of St. John lie within the national park. Swimming among the reefs of many colors and hues, I observe coral rising like trees, mountains, and spires, the violet-hued sea fans swaying in the current, the anemones carpeting the reef like shrubbery. I follow schools of brilliant fish gliding through sunlit waters or resting on stony branches.

Diving at night offers different perspectives, for at night the reef comes alive with the little coral animals that avoid daylight, thrusting out their tentacled heads to feed on plankton. Other reef creatures respond to darkness too, emerging from crevices and grottoes that serve as daylight shelter.

The pattern of life changes as one moves upward from the sea. In traveling about the island to the rainy mountaintops, I note the swift transition in vegetation; few areas anywhere span so wide a range, from the sea grape shading the pale coral strand to lush broadleaf evergreens. Land birds are abundant, with a few water birds along the shores. From a distance the wooded hills remind me of the New England countryside, but then I see coconut-laden palms, breadfruit, soursop, wild orange trees, and little plants and vines bearing local botanical names like clashie melashi,

CINNAMON BAY

eyebright, and better man better. From Maney Peak, elevation 1,147 feet, I see the other U.S. and all the British Virgin Islands—the latter still unspoiled—spread over the brilliant, calm sea.

Columbus discovered the islands and named them after the 11,000 virgins of martyred St. Ursula. At that time St. John was inhabited by Carib Indians who left behind petroglyphs that still fascinate archaeologists. Dutch, English, Spanish, and French adventurers followed. Then came the Danes, who established a sometime prosperous society based on sugar production. On high, breezy hills I visit the ruins of plantation houses, stone boundary walls, and ghostly old sugar mills dating back to the early eighteenth century. The United States bought St. John and the larger St. Thomas and St. Croix islands from Denmark in 1917 solely to keep the Germans out of the Caribbean.

When Virgin Islands National Park was established in 1956, it was none too soon. This small, priceless tropical fragment of our nation occupies about three-fourths of St. John (which is only nine miles long and five miles wide). With the unending discovery and commercial development of one "unspoiled" Caribbean island after another, St. John is one of the very few islands where sparkling beaches and bays, coral reefs, pleasant valleys, and forested mountains are still preserved.

RUINS OF ANNABERG ESTATE

TRUNK BAY

The Newest Parks

IN 1980, CONGRESS DESIGNATED FOR PROTECTION AS NATIONAL PARKS, MONUMENTS, PRESERVES, WILDLIFE refuges, national forests, and wild and scenic rivers, a total of more than 104 million acres —the largest land area protected by any single piece of conservation legislation.

That law, the Alaska National Interest Lands Conservation Act, or ANILCA, added 43,588,000 acres to the National Park System, including some of the most glorious landscapes on earth. Five spectacular new national parks—Gates of the Arctic, Kenai Fjords, Kobuk Valley, Lake Clark, and Wrangell-St. Elias—were established. Two national monuments—Glacier Bay and Katmai—were enlarged and redesignated as national parks. Mount McKinley National Park also was enlarged and renamed Denali National Park.

Besides these units, ANILCA directed the establishment of important national monuments and preserves. These include Aniakchak, extending from the Alaskan mainland toward the Aleutians, a land of tundra, lakes, rivers and volcanic peaks, with one of the world's largest calderas (or collapsed summits); Bering Land Bridge, gateway to the New World, containing immense deposits left by migrating prehistoric hunters; Cape Krusenstern, where the ocean level rose to submerge the Bering land bridge that once linked Alaska with Asia; and Noatak, a major portion of the largest untouched river basin in America, embracing much of the corridor of the storied Yukon, Mississippi of the North, and the entire drainage of the wild Charley River.

These areas all are administered by the National Park Service. I should also mention two other national monuments, Misty Fjords and Admiralty Island, both in southeastern Alaska, that are part of Tongass National Forest. No matter, all were chosen because they are components of the last remaining wilderness in North America. They are still free from human interference, little altered by mechanical change—a field laboratory of natural plant and animal communities, sheer inspiration to humankind.

But for how long? National parks in Alaska were resisted by various groups, principally for self-serving commercial reasons. Park wildlife lacks adequate protection from wildlife poachers. Pressures continue for incompatible developments *within* park boundaries. Still, Americans have a way of rallying to a cause when their support is most needed. That, it is hoped, will prove the case.

All national parks are a little like the news, which doesn't happen until someone makes it happen. A national park comes into being only when someone wants it badly enough.

That someone usually is a private citizen. Read the story of Biscayne National Park (starting on page 155), which tells how a mere handful organized a group called Safe Progress. Its members knew very little about parks when they started, but they had a feel for natural beauty and a desire to save what they could of it.

One of them was a friend of mine, Lane Guthrie, an airline pilot based in Miami (also father of Janet Guthrie, celebrated as the first woman driver to race in the Indianapolis 500). As Lane flew back and forth across the country, he observed polluted skies and unappealing sights below. He remembered what southern Florida was like in earlier, more natural days. On one flight, Lane refused to dump his excess fuel over Miami. He got in trouble with the airline, but only for a little while. Many people cheered his stand on principle; they got to thinking prudently of saving rather than wasting.

At the outset, Biscayne-park advocates thought they were saving scenery. Later they learned the islands and islets in question supported stands of rare mahogany and lignum vitae and species of ferns and palms thought to be extinct. Once they got their national park, the protection of the area was enhanced by nearby Key Largo Coral Reef National Marine Sanctuary, with 100 square miles of underwater life.

The story was the same in California, where the 1969 oil spill off Santa Barbara stirred public concern and awareness of the Channel Islands as a natural wonderland, all the more remarkable for its proximity to the Los Angeles megalopolis.

In 1980, when the former national monument was redesignated as a national park, yet another action designated surrounding waters as the first marine sanctuary on the Pacific Coast, to be kept free of oil and gas drilling.

The same awareness and involvement are manifest in the Santa Monica Mountains, which stretch 50 miles westward from Griffith Park, in downtown Los Angeles, to Point Mugu, on the Pacific Coast. In 1978, following 15 years of effort, Santa Monica Mountains National Recreation Area was established by Congress. It may not be called "national park," yet it preserves and protects choice fragments of mountain and seashore —and that's what counts.

Kenai Fjords National Park

Cruising the fjords aboard a sturdy old motor-powered sailer, I am treated to the kind of magnificent vistas one envisions in Norway, but I doubt that anything in Norway can match the outer flanks of the Kenai Peninsula. Here rock rises thousands of feet from the sea to the snowy peaks of the Harding Ice Field, which spreads over an area almost as large as Rhode Island.

In misty Resurrection Bay, largest of the fjords, whales, porpoises, seals, and sea otters

GLACIER IN THE BROOKS RANGE

feel at home among the sea arches, caves, and cliffs. The rhythm of life in this bay is constantly being reshaped by the pounding energy of incoming tides.

Along with marine mammals, Aialik Bay and Harris Bay harbor immense concentrations of seabirds, which favor the fractured cliff ledges and small islands. The new national park covers 570,000 acres, with choice portions accessible by land. From Seward I drive to Exit Glacier to observe and explore the river of ice flowing down from the Harding Ice Field. The retreating glacier exposes scoured bedrock, opening the way for new vegetation and wildlife. Mountaintops of the central ice core are fittingly called *nunataks*, a lovely native word that means "lonely peaks."

Gates of the Arctic National Park

In late August I find that the first frosts have reached the deep, silent valleys of the Brooks Range before me and have turned grasses, willow and birch, lichen and sedge into a pattern of russet and gold. The colors match the setting of granite peaks and knifelike ridges north of Fairbanks and of the Arctic Circle. The dramatic long valleys, immense in their solitude, fill with the sound of migrating caribou and then fall silent once more. The Arctic strikes me as a pleasing land for those

willing to understand and appreciate it on its own terms.

This new national park and the bordering national preserve cover 7,952,000 acres of majestic mountains, lakes, and rivers. The idea of setting aside this vast area came from the late Robert Marshall, whose writings on exploring Alaska's wilderness chart a course for the adventurous to follow. From 1929 to 1939, he conducted research around the headwaters of the Koyukuk River, recording his experience in *Arctic Wilderness*, a book still available and well worth reading.

Since he respected Eskimos and their ways, I think of Bob Marshall when I arrive at Anaktuvuk Pass, a village within the park. The Anaktuvuk are subsistence hunters, dependent on migrating caribou.

151

Glacier Bay
National Park

Deep in the bay a whale becomes visible from the cruise boat, lifting itself completely out of the water, bending in a graceful arc, and plunging below the surface. Such pleasures of the eye are purely unscheduled, but in the course of three different visits to the 50-mile-long bay, near Juneau in southeast Alaska, I have learned to expect something memorable. The waters are flecked with icebergs and dotted with islands and rocks teeming with birds —from eagles to cormorants and puffins— while glaciers in every stage of development reach the water's edge at narrow, fjord-like inlets, often with cliffs at least 100 feet high. The new national park (formerly a national monument) and preserve of 3,385,000 acres embrace the Fairweather Range, culminating in 15,320-foot-high Mount Fairweather, a snowy beacon that presents a challenge to climbers.

GLACIER BAY

KATMAI FISHING STREAM

Katmai
National Park

For many years Katmai National Monument was known as the largest unit of the National Park System and as the site of the violent 1912 volcanic eruption in what later became known as the Valley of Ten Thousand Smokes. As a national park and national preserve of 4,268,000 acres, it deserves to be known on other counts as well. Here on the Alaska Peninsula west of Anchorage, some of the largest brown bears thrive in company with moose, wolf, smaller mammals, and red salmon. Waterbirds and songbirds are abundant and varied. Fishermen have long favored Katmai's lakes and streams, but it doesn't take a rod and reel to appreciate beauty spots like the Brooks River and Kulik Lake and make the most of them.

Kobuk Valley National Park

Walking through golden sand dunes is an exercise one would hardly anticipate 40 miles north of the Arctic Circle; yet here I find myself in the seemingly misplaced Great Kobuk Sand Dunes, which spread over 25 square miles. The rolling dunes, rising as high as 100 feet, are only one part of the broad basin of the Kobuk River, which flows for 300 miles from the south flank of the Brooks Range, picking up the waters of at least 50 tributaries before emptying into Kotzebue Sound and the Chukchi Sea. To the canoeist the river seems like a series of lakes, with abundant opportunities to fish, to observe the wildlife, and to enjoy solitude amid space unspoiled.

The national park of 1,710,000 acres embraces several Eskimo villages strung along the Kobuk. Eskimos have lived here as long as man has been on this continent. They await the twice-yearly migrations of the caribou, which advance in waves through mountain passes to forage on the tundra plains. Furnishing meat and hides to the Eskimo, caribou are part of an earthscape harmony.

GREAT KOBUK SAND DUNES

Lake Clark National Park

Chuck Hornberger and I drift downstream in his small boat on the Chulitna River, slipping up on a moose, and then a beaver. We might just as easily encounter eagles, falcons, ducks, swans, or songbirds, all of which dwell here. Chuck and his wife, a former teacher, own and operate Koksetna Lodge at the edge of Lake Clark, a small and simple facility that they built with their own hands in a setting of majestic peaks, glacial valleys, and sparkling lakes and streams. They typify a breed: guides, owners of small resorts, and boat owners who love Alaska as it is and are ready to help visitors grasp its meaning.

"One thing we have here in great quantity is quiet," says Chuck. His remark is a reminder of Koksetna's self-reliant wilderness way of life (which even includes the windmill Chuck ingeniously installed for electric power). And what a place to enjoy it, with 3,650,000 acres of natural splendor in the national park and preserve, 150 miles west of Anchorage.

LAKE CLARK

WRANGELL MOUNTAINS

Wrangell–St. Elias National Park

Hiking uphill from the old mining town of McCarthy, I find summer wildflowers and berries covering the countryside and may have a chance to spot (at least with binoculars) Dall sheep, moose, or bear. I feel overwhelmed with what Alaska has to offer as our greatest wildlife sanctuary. Alaska's wilderness, in fact, represents a form of wealth, a national treasure, that is disappearing throughout the world. Thus it makes sense that this national park and preserve, covering 12,318,000 acres, should be the largest anywhere on earth. Here, in south central Alaska, I can see the greatest concentration of high peaks on the continent (including Mount St. Elias, third-highest peak), with their massive glaciers, snowfields, and waterfalls that yield into roaring rivers. McCarthy and neighboring Kennicott are colorful reminders of yesterday's mining history, but the future of the Wrangells surely must be in their beauty. While absorbing the wonders of this outdoor kingdom, I feel the rightness of setting aside this portion of the earth, without a price tag.

PELICANS LANDING

Biscayne National Park

THE WINDS ARE BLOWING, FRESH- ENING THE WHITECAPS. THE WA- TER IS A LITTLE TOO ROUGH, ALAS, to cruise out to the coral reefs as we had planned. Jim Tilmant, the park biologist, points the boat into Hurricane Creek instead. This proves a wise choice, since the creek is protected and calm, lined with a pleasant forest of red mangrove in the lee of Old Rhodes Key. And here we snorkel in watery nurseries of marine life.

Rich and varied sea grasses bend with the gentle current. The creek is less than ten feet deep, with occasional pools extending to about 15 feet. The waters are alive with juvenile snappers and grunts, which feed and grow here before heading for the offshore reefs and deeper water, and with brilliant-colored parrot fish, angelfish, and wrasses.

This national park, as Jim has explained, protects three significant, related biological systems. Hurricane Creek typifies one of them —shallow Biscayne Bay, the aquatic nursery. The others are the offshore islands, or keys, with their distinctive tropical vegetation, and the coral reef on the Atlantic side, the sanc- tuary of many types of corals, sponges, sea grasses, shellfish, crabs, starfish, and reef fish —a complex of life that is simply not found elsewhere in America.

When we resume our travels by boat and reach Elliott Key, the major island (seven miles across the Bay from Convoy Point, park head- quarters on the mainland), I begin to appre- ciate more fully the value of Biscayne National Park as an idea as well as a place.

During the 1960s, as I learn, Elliott Key was still privately held, and there were dreams of making it and nearby islands into another Miami Beach. Most of it was subdivided and lots were sold. In this same period a "sub- marginal" tract on the mainland was rezoned to allow Daniel K. Ludwig, the shipping and oil king, to build a refinery.

These developments stirred the concern of biologists, engineers, and outdoor-minded Flo- ridians. For one thing, Biscayne Bay is an enclosed body where prevailing winds blow onshore, with industrial wastes endangering parks, yacht clubs, homes, and hotels. For an- other, unlike the northern half of the Bay, bordering urbanized Miami and Miami Beach, the southern half still remained unspoiled.

Starting as a mere handful, the citizens or- ganized a group called "Safe Progress." They studied one potential course of action after another, sending speakers to every civic club and media outlet that would have one. It was an uphill battle against promises of jobs and increased tax revenues, yet in due course pop- ular feeling swung behind Safe Progress and preservation.

The county commissioners took a fresh look of their own and asked the Department of the Interior to study the south bay and off- shore "Islandia" as a possible national park. The developers of Elliott Key were so incensed that they defiantly bulldozed a path, still clearly evident, the entire length of the island, barely missing a stand of rare palms.

"We are losing the battle to keep America beautiful," Stewart L. Udall, then Secretary of the Interior, told the park advocates when he came to inspect the scene. "You must band together to make a stronger fight. It's not cheap or easy. But persist." In 1968, as a result of continued efforts, Biscayne National Monu- ment was established, covering 96,000 acres dominated by water and reef. In 1980 the monument was enlarged to 175,700 acres, in- cluding significant islands and mainland man- groves, and reclassified as a national park.

Everywhere I look this action is one to cheer. The towers of Miami Beach are visible but seem a world apart from this haven for boaters, birders, fishermen, and divers.

The islands and islets, numbering more than 30, support stands of rare mahogany and lignum vitae, and species of ferns and palms that had been thought extinct. The tropical forests shelter colorful migratory birds flying to and from the Caribbean and beyond.

As for the reefs, the only living coral reefs in the continental United States are found along the crescent-shaped arc of the Florida Keys. Now Biscayne National Park and John Pennekamp Coral Reef State Park, just south of it, form an unbroken sanctuary.

Best of all, Biscayne National Park serves as a living laboratory where city school- children come to learn about the marvels that have been saved for them.

OVERLEAF: BISCAYNE CORAL AND SEA LIFE >

CALIFORNIA

Channel Islands National Park

THE SIGHT OF SEA LIONS AND FUR SEALS, NUMEROUS AND DENSE, AS THEY MIGHT HAVE BEEN 500 YEARS ago, long before the first explorers arrived, makes me feel that Point Bennett, on San Miguel Island, must surely offer one of the world's outstanding wildlife displays.

We watch from a respectful distance, focusing binoculars on the huge elephant seals, weighing up to 5,000 pounds or more, marked by the prominent snout, or proboscis, that brings the term "elephant" to mind. These great mammals of the sea, though now rare, are safe here in the Channel Islands. San Miguel, in fact (where visitors may go only with written permission from park headquarters), provides sanctuary to more species of pinnipeds—aquatic mammals whose limbs have evolved into flippers—than are found at any other single location on earth. Besides the elephant seal, these include the only breeding colony of northern fur seal south of Alaska, the California sea lion, the Steller sea lion, the harbor seal, and the Guadalupe fur seal.

San Miguel, westernmost of the Channel Islands, is misty and moody, often shrouded in fog and sometimes in storm. As I walk with Bill Ehorn, the park superintendent, I see that wind-driven sand covers much of the island, with calcified root castings of ancient trees forming "caliche forests" in the dunes. Bill points out midden sites—refuse dumps of shells, bones, and tools—and vestiges of little settlements left by the Chumash Indians, significant in science because of their abundance and antiquity.

Everywhere on the Channel Islands I am reminded of the Galápagos, off the coast of Ecuador. Both groups are living witness to land-forming explosions of the floor of the Pacific, with volcanic summits rising out of the sea and formations of lava, cinder, and ash evident in cliffs, canyons, and beaches. The Galápagos have their iguanas, tortoises, flightless birds, and their Darwin legacy, that is true, but the Channel Islands support an equally rich concentration of life.

I learn that the waters south of San Miguel and Santa Rosa have lately been determined to be a major migration pathway for large species of whales, including the endangered humpback, the extremely rare blue, and the finback and sei. The lush undisturbed kelp beds and plankton serve as food for mollusks, crustaceans, and fish, which in turn support seabirds, dolphins, porpoises, and whales.

While the Galápagos lie 600 miles off the coast of Ecuador, the Channel Islands are a natural wonderland at the back door of booming Southern California. The eight islands are only ten to 70 miles from the mainland of which they may once have been part—an extension of the Santa Monica Mountains broken away by the sea in geological history.

Since 1938 two islands of the northern group, Anacapa and Santa Barbara, have been protected as a national monument. With the 1969 oil spill off the prominent coastal resort of Santa Barbara, however, public concern intensified for the islands and the waters around them. Consequently San Miguel, formerly administered by the Navy, was added to the monument.

Then in 1970 Dr. Carey Stanton, owner of a substantial portion of Santa Cruz Island, entered into an agreement with the Nature Conservancy, aimed at insuring protection of cliffs, beaches, rocky headlands, and tidepools—a living example of primeval America. The conservancy's Santa Cruz Island project was launched with a gift of land plus the purchase of 54,500 acres. Among the attractions of Santa Cruz are peaks rising over 2,000 feet, spectacular sea caves, and 140 species of land birds. President Carter designated a six-mile area around the island as the marine sanctuary on the Pacific Coast, to be kept free of any drilling for oil and gas.

On Anacapa Island, closest to the mainland (11 miles from Oxnard), I follow the nature trail, observing tidepools rich in multicolored anemones, sea urchins, and myriad other life forms. I see the effect of waves crashing onto old mountaintops in arches, blowholes, caves, and sea cliffs, and in the black sand beaches composed of particles of ancient lava. On land, dense stands of giant coreopsis, a striking tree-like sunflower, again suggest the Galápagos.

Birds, too, are abundant in the Channel Islands as in the Galápagos, including gulls, cormorants, oyster catchers, and brown pelicans, a species that is rebounding from near-extinction in a sanctuary on West Anacapa. Some species roost on the California mainland but depend on the Channel Islands for breeding and nesting, thus re-creating a scene of long ago when the world was fresh and new, and all along the coast the cliffs teemed with bird colonies, the rocky beaches with seals and sea lions, and the offshore kelp beds with sea otters. The Channel Islands are not exactly easy to reach, but the very sight of them from anywhere in urbanized Southern California brings a sense of pleasure.

SEA LIONS (BELOW) AND LANDSCAPE (RIGHT), SAN MIGUEL ISLAND